T3-BEA-620

Great Misadventures

Great Misadventures

Bad Ideas That Led to Big Disasters

PEGGY SAARI

EDITED BY BETZ DES CHENES

VOLUME THREE: MILITARY

Detroit • London

Great Misadventures: Bad Ideas That Led to Big Disasters

Peggy Saari

Staff

Elizabeth Des Chenes, *U·X·L Senior Editor*
Carol DeKane Nagel, *U·X·L Managing Editor*
Thomas L. Romig, *U·X·L Publisher*

Margaret Chamberlain, *Permissions Specialist (Pictures)*

Mary Beth Trimper, *Production Director*
Evi Seoud, *Assistant Production Manager*
Deborah Milliken, *Production Assistant*

Cynthia Baldwin, *Product Design Manager*
Michelle Dimercurio, *Art Director*
Linda Mahoney, *Typesetting*

Library of Congress Cataloging-in-Publication Data

Great Misadventures: Bad Ideas That Led to Big Disasters/ Peggy Saari, editor
v. cm.
Includes bibliographical references.
Summary: Explores 100 historical, political, military, and social events where human error has led to disaster.
ISBN 0-7876-2798-4 (set: alk. paper). — ISBN 0-7876-2799-2 (v. 1: alk. paper) — ISBN 0-7876-2800-X (v. 2: alk. paper) — ISBN 0-7876-2801-8 (v. 3: alk paper) — ISBN 0-7876-2802-6 (v. 4: alk. paper)
1. History—Miscellanea—Juvenile literature. 2. Disasters—Juvenile literature. [1. Disasters. 2. History—Miscellanea]
I. Saari, Peggy.
D24 G64 1998
904—dc21 98-13811
CIP

∞™ This book is printed on acid-free paper that meets the minimum requirements of American National Standard for information Sciences—Permanence Paper for Printed Library Materials, ANSI Z39.48-1984.

Printed in the United States of America

10 9 8 7 6 5 4 3 2 1

Contents

VOLUME THREE: MILITARY

VOLUME FOUR: SOCIETY

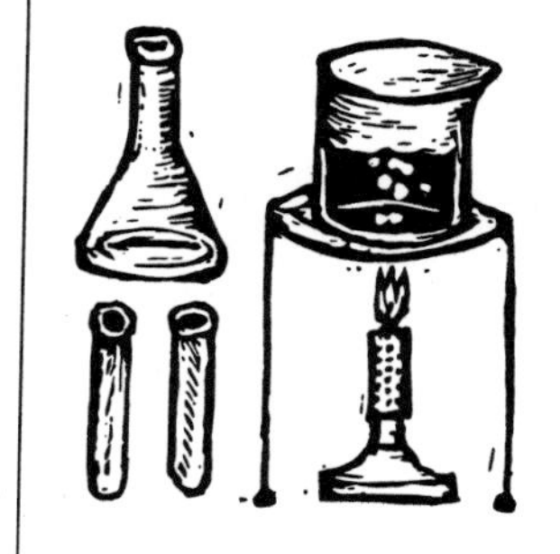

Reader's Guide

Great Misadventures: Bad Ideas That Led to Big Disasters presents 100 stories of human error, greed, and poor judgment that span history from ancient times through the present. Each entry, whether on an infamous adventure, a technological failure, a deadly battle, or a social calamity, offers historical background and a vivid description of the event, together with a discussion about why the misadventure is significant.

In many cases, a misadventure had a positive outcome—laws were enacted, failure led to progress, the protagonist became a national hero—but in others, death or destruction were the only result. It is disillusioning to learn, for example, that a great explorer committed atrocities, or that a well-known celebrity was a liar. It is equally disturbing to discover that incompetent leaders caused needless loss of life in wars, or that cutting-edge technology was sometimes useless or even dangerous. The goal of *Great Misadventures* is to show that success can also involve failure, triumph can encompass defeat, and human beings are inspired by self-interest as often as they are motivated by selflessness.

Format

The *Great Misadventures* entries are arranged chronologically within four subject volumes: Exploration and Adventure, Science and Technology, Military, and Society. Cross references direct users to related entries throughout the four-volume set, while sources for further reference at the end of each entry offer more information on featured people and events. Call-out boxes present biographical profiles and fascinating facts, and more than 220 black-and-white photographs, illustrations, and maps help illuminate the text. Each volume contains an annotated table of contents, a timeline of important events, and a cumulative index.

Comments and Suggestions

We welcome your comments and suggestions for subjects to feature in future editions of *Great Misadventures.* Please write: Editors, *Great Misadventures,* U•X•L, 27500 Drake Rd., Farmington Hills, Michigan, 48331–3535; call toll-free: 800–877–4253; or fax 1–800–414–5043.

Timeline

415 B.C. Athenian naval commander Alcibiades is defeated during an assault on Syracuse.

325 B.C. Macedonian leader Alexander the Great leads a tragic expedition across the Gedrosia desert.

30 B.C. Egyptian queen Cleopatra commits suicide.

1118 French philosopher Peter Abelard begins a tragic love affair with his student Hëloise.

1187 Christian Crusaders lose the Battle of Hattin to the Muslims.

1212 Stephen of Cloyes, a French shepherd boy, leads the ill-fated Children's Crusade.

1498 Italian explorer Christopher Columbus begins his rule of Hispaniola.

c. 1500 The Norse settlement in Greenland is abandoned.

1533 Spanish conquistador Pedro de Alvarado leads a disastrous trek across the Andes.

1541 Spanish conquistador Francisco Vázquez de Coronado fails to find the Seven Cities of Cibola.

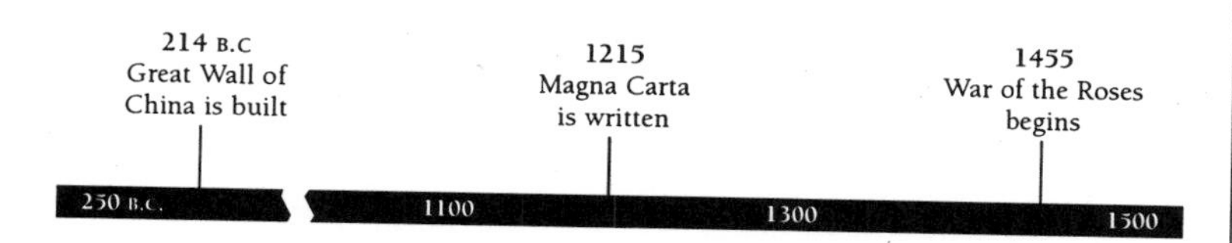

1591 English colonists disappear from the Roanoke settlement.

1597 Dutch explorer Willem Barents dies in a failed attempt to find a northeast sea passage to Asia.

1605 English Roman Catholics fail to blow up Parliament as part of the Gunpowder Plot.

1618 English explorer Sir Walter Raleigh is beheaded for disobeying King James I.

1625 The British fleet is defeated in a disastrous misadventure at the port of Cádiz, Spain.

1687 French explorer René-Robert de La Salle is killed by his own men.

1709 The Swedish army loses the Battle of Poltava because of a squabble between two of its commanders.

1776 Hessian colonel Johann Gottlieb Rall loses the Battle of Trenton when he underestimates rebel troop strength.

1779 English explorer James Cook is murdered by angry Hawaiian islanders.

1806 Scottish explorer Mungo Park drowns during an expedition on the Niger River.

1811 Rebellious English textile workers calling themselves "Luddites" begin a failed uprising against the Industrial Revolution.

1812 Poor leadership by American general William Hull leads to the Fall of Detroit during the War of 1812.

1815 French leader Napoléon Bonaparte is defeated by British forces at the Battle of Waterloo.

1831 African American slave Nat Turner leads the failed Southampton Insurrection.

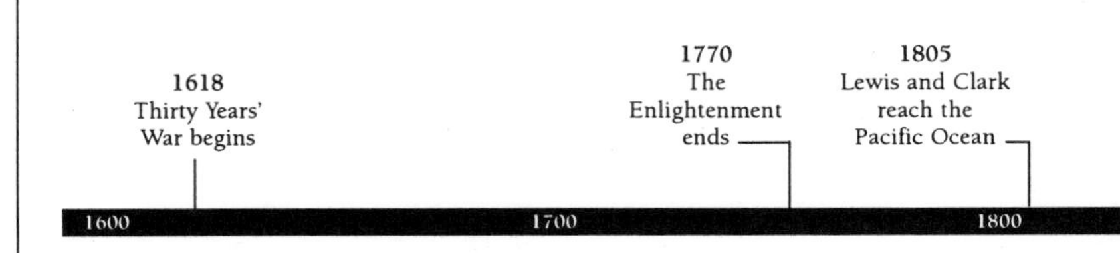

1844 Canadian trapper Peter Skene Ogden explores territory for Britain that is later lost to the United States in a land dispute.

1846 Donner Party members resort to cannibalism after being trapped in the Sierra Nevada.

1847 British explorer John Franklin is lost at sea during his search for the Northwest Passage.

1855 Deprivations during the Crimean War lead to an overwhelming number of deaths among British soldiers.

1859 Abolitionist John Brown stages a failed raid on the federal arsenal at Harpers Ferry, Virginia.

1861 Australian explorers Robert O'Hara Burke and William John Wills starve to death during their transcontinental expedition.

1863 Confederate general George Edward Pickett marches his troops to certain death at the Battle of Gettysburg.

1863 The African American 54th Massachusetts Regiment stages an heroic but unsuccessful assault on Fort Wagner, South Carolina.

1870 Paraguay's male population is reduced by almost ninety percent during the "War of the Triple Alliance."

1873 British missionary and explorer David Livingstone dies during his final adventure in Africa.

1873 French explorer Francis Garnier makes a tactical error that ends French control of the Vietnamese city of Hanoi.

1876 The 7th Cavalry is annihilated by Sioux and Cheyenne warriors at the Battle of Little BigHorn.

1881 American explorer George Washington De Long and his crew are lost while attempting to find a route to the North Pole through the Bering Strait.

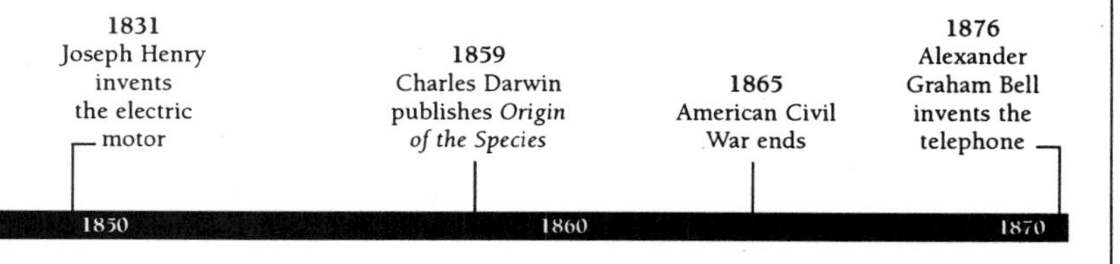

1908 American explorer Frederick Albert Cook claims to be the first man to reach the North Pole.

1911 One hundred and forty-six immigrant workers perish in the Triangle Shirtwaist Company fire in New York City.

1912 British explorer Robert Falcon Scott and his party freeze to death on their return trip from the South Pole.

1912 The luxury ocean liner *Titanic* sinks after hitting an iceberg.

1915 Poor leadership and bad communication leads to high Allied casualties at the Battle of Gallipoli.

1916 Irish revolutionaries stage the unsuccessful Easter Rising.

1919 A steel tank containing 12,000 tons of molasses bursts open in Boston, Massachusetts, and kills twenty-one people.

1919 British troops kill 379 unarmed Indian protestors during the Amritsar Massacre.

1920 Seven Chicago White Sox players are banned from playing baseball for their role in the "Black Sox" betting scandal.

1928 Italian pilot Umberto Nobile crashes the airship *Italia* during a flight to the North Pole.

1934 The Dionne quintuplets are born in Canada and soon become a tourist and media attraction.

1937 American aviator Amelia Earhart and her navigator Fred Noonan are lost on a flight across the Pacific Ocean.

1937 The airship *Hindenberg* explodes after landing in Lakehurst, New Jersey.

1938 The *War of the Worlds* radio broadcast about a fictional Martian invasion causes widespread public panic.

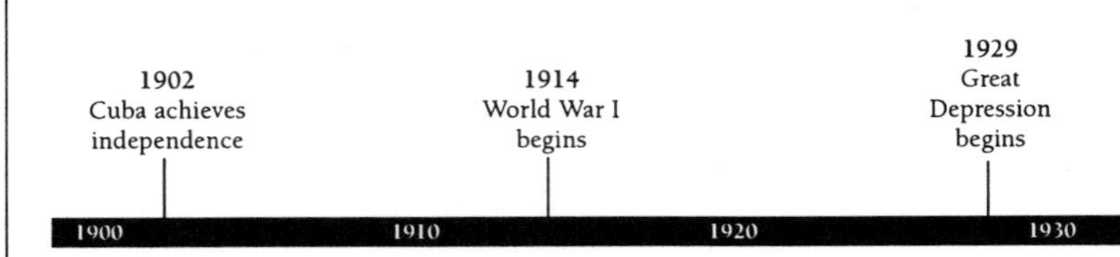

1941 German leader Adolf Hitler launches Operation Barbarossa, his failed invasion of Russia.

1944 The Japanese navy and air force stage a futile kamikaze attack at the Battle of Leyte Gulf.

1947 American inventor Howard Hughes flies his *Spruce Goose* seaplane for ninety seconds.

1950 U.S. senator Joseph McCarthy launches his four-year search for Communist infiltrators.

1951 U.S. general Douglas MacArthur is relieved of his command during the Korean War.

1953 Julius and Ethel Rosenberg become the first U.S. citizens to be executed for espionage.

1956 A United Airlines DC-7 and a TWA Constellation collide in empty air space over the Grand Canyon.

1956 American college instructor Charles Van Doren becomes involved in the *Twenty-One* quiz show scandal.

1961 CIA-trained Cuban refugees fail to overthrow dictator Fidel Castro during the Bay of Pigs invasion.

1961 The U.S. Air Force begins spraying the defoliant Agent Orange in Vietnam.

1969 General Motors discontinues production of the controversial Chevrolet Corvair, America's first rear-engine automobile.

1970 American astronauts abort the *Apollo 13* mission to the Moon.

1972 A failed burglary at the offices of the Democratic National Committee sets the stage for the Watergate scandal.

1973 The United States ends its long and disastrous military involvement in the Vietnam War.

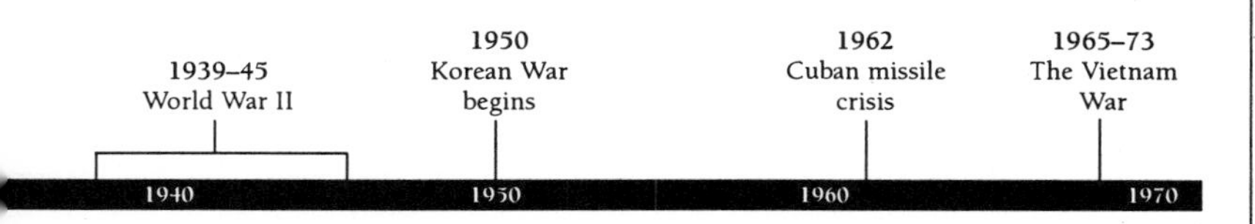

1978 The Ford Motor Company recalls 1.4 million Pinto automobiles after several fatal rear-impact collisions.

1979 The Three Mile Island nuclear power plant in Pennsylvania has an accidental meltdown.

1980 Love Canal, New York, is evacuated after years of toxic waste dumping make this residential area uninhabitable.

1980 Fire protection systems fail to prevent a blaze from engulfing the MGM Grand Hotel in Las Vegas, Nevada.

1980 U.S. military forces stage an aborted rescue of American hostages in Tehran, Iran.

1983 Artificial heart recipient Barney Clark dies 112 days after his historic surgery.

1983 The infamous copper mining "Pit" in Butte, Montana is closed.

1984 A poisonous gas cloud escapes from the Union Carbide chemical plant in Bhopal, India, killing thousands of people.

1986 Two mammoth explosions blow apart Unit 4 of the Chernobyl nuclear power plant in the Ukraine.

1986 The entire flight crew dies when the space shuttle *Challenger* explodes after launch.

1989 The oil tanker Exxon *Valdez* runs aground in Alaska, spilling 10.8 million gallons of crude oil and polluting 1,500 miles of shoreline.

1991 U.S. diplomatic failures help trigger the Persian Gulf War.

1992 Silicone breast implants are banned by the Food and Drug Administration.

1992 John Gotti, the "Teflon Don," is sentenced to life in prison after his underboss, Sammy "the Bull" Gravano, testifies against the Gambino crime family.

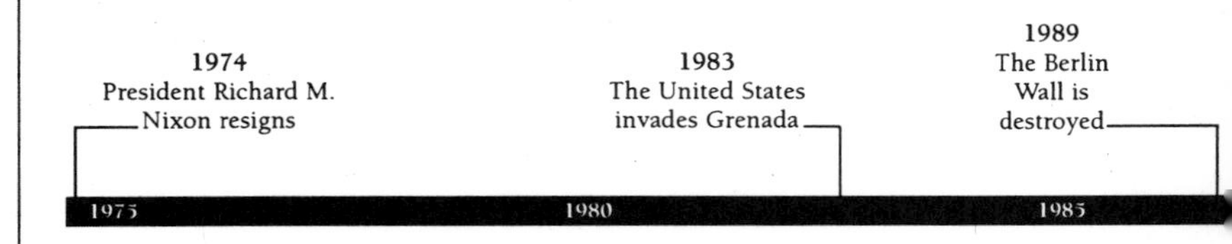

1992 American adventurer Christopher McCandless starves to death during an Alaskan wilderness trek.

1993 The U.S. Congress ends funding for the Superconductor Super Collider.

1994 U.S. figure skater Tanya Harding is implicated in an assault on fellow skater Nancy Kerrigan.

1994 CIA agent Aldrich Ames is convicted of spying for the Soviet Union.

1995 Twelve people die and thousands are injured in a nerve gas attack in Tokyo, Japan.

1995 English stock trader Nicholas Leeson triggers the collapse of Barings PLC.

1995 The controversial Denver International Airport in Colorado finally opens for business.

1996 The British government orders the slaughter of thousands of cattle infected with mad cow disease.

1996 Seven-year-old American pilot Jessica Dubroff dies while trying to set an aviation record.

1996 Seven climbers perish during a blizzard on Mount Everest.

1997 The MRTA hostage crisis at the Japanese embassy in Lima, Peru, reaches a violent climax.

1997 The Canadian Bre-X mining company is shut down after the world's largest "gold discovery" proves to be a hoax.

1997 American scientist Karen Wetterhahn dies after being exposed to liguid mercury during a laboratory experiment.

1998 Federal Aviation Administration technicians conclude that the mainframe computer used in the nation's largest air traffic control centers is "Year 2000" compliant.

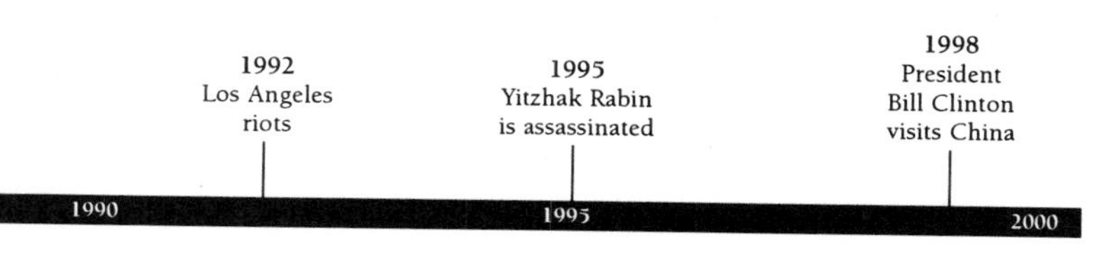

Great Misadventures

The Fall of Athens

415 B.C TO 413 B.C.

Alcibiades's treachery was instrumental in the defeat of the magnificent Athenian fleet.

During the Peloponnesian War, in 415 B.C, the Greek city-state of Athens began a naval attack on Syracuse, a Greek city-state in present-day Sicily, Italy. The assault ended in failure. Led by the great but unscrupulous commander Alcibiades (450 B.C.–404 B.C.), the Athenian fleet was the largest ever assembled in the ancient world. With such a strong force, Athenian leaders knew they could win the battle if Syracuse did not receive military support from Sparta, Athens's enemy. What the Athenians did not predict was the treachery of Alcibiades and the incompetence of another Athenian commander, Nicias (died 413 B.C.). Both of these men were instrumental in the defeat of the magnificent Athenian fleet. As a result, the ambitious naval expedition turned into a huge misadventure that led to the downfall of Athens.

The Peloponnesian War

The Peloponnesian War (431 B.C.–404 B.C.) was a struggle for political power between the Greek city-states of Athens and Sparta. (A city-state was an independent political unit that consisted of a city and the surrounding countryside. There were several hundred city-states in ancient Greece.) Athens had a democratic form of government under which rulers were elected by the people. With the most powerful navy in the ancient

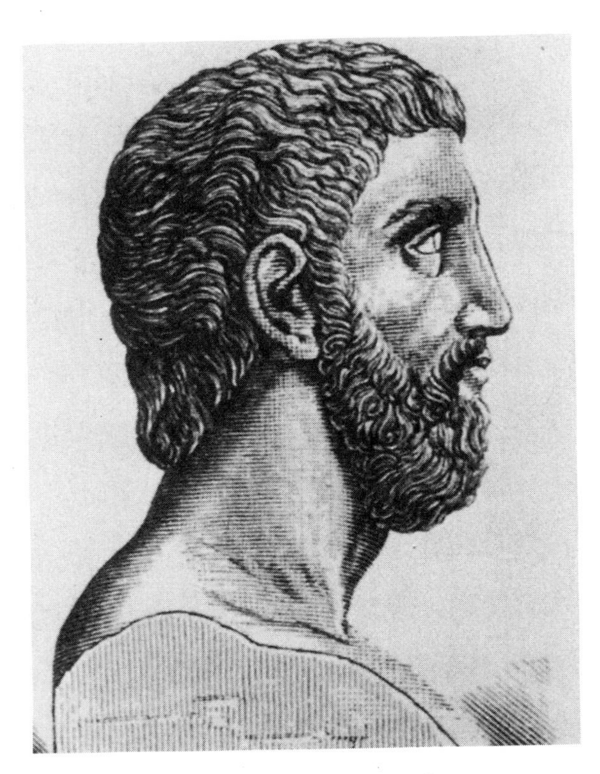

A former student of the Greek philosopher Socrates, Alcibiades eventually became greedy for political power and turned against his tutor.

world, Athens protected neighboring democratic city-states. Sparta was an empire ruled by an oligarchy (small group) called the "Spartiates" who were completely devoted to war. Trained from birth to become soldiers at age twenty, Spartan men served in the military until age sixty. Spartan women also fought in battle.

During the Persian Wars (500 B.C.–449 B.C) Sparta led the Peloponnesian League in an alliance with Athens, which headed the Delian League. Both leagues were confederations (political unions) of Greek city-states. The Peloponnesian War began in 431 B.C. when the Spartans invaded Attica, a region around Athens, in a drive to replace democratic governments with the oligarchy system. Athenian and Spartan forces met at the battle of Syracuse (415 B.C.–413 B.C.), which resulted in the downfall of Athens as a major power. The war ended in 404 B.C. when the Spartan general Lysander established an oligarchy called the "Thirty Tyrants" in Athens.

Position becomes precarious

The Athenian navy, which was commanded by the famous generals Alcibiades and Lymarchus, was a powerful force during the Peloponnesian War. In 415 B.C., Alcibiades persuaded Athenian leaders to let him mount an expedition to invade Syracuse. By that time, however, the navy had been at war for fifteen years and its resources were running low. Consequently, Athens had to recruit mercenaries (hired soldiers) to support Alcibiades's grand scheme. Although Alcibiades was not assured of assistance from Athenian allies in Sicily and Italy, he continued toward Syracuse because he was too proud to return home without a victory.

Even though Alcibiades managed to acquire a naval base in the Sicilian city of Catana, he could not persuade other allies to join his campaign. Not only did this lack of support severely weaken the Athenian navy, it gave Syracuse time to prepare for the impending battle. Nevertheless, the Athenians managed to set up a blockade around Syracuse.

Then the Athenian fleet was dealt a fatal blow. Alcibiades was accused of impiety (lack of proper respect) for vandalizing religious statues and he had to return to Athens to stand trial. (Historians speculate that he was innocent of the charges.) Fearing execution, Alcibiades fled to Sparta and convinced the Spartan king Agis II to support Syracuse in the battle against Athens. The Athenian navy was now in even greater jeopardy, with its strongest leader having defected to the other side. To make matters worse, after Alcibiades left Athens he was replaced by Nicias, a mediocre and superstitious military leader. If the Athenian navy lost Lymarchus—its only remaining hope—it would have to rely on Nicias, who was unfit for command.

Victory becomes impossible

Meanwhile, the Athenians continued their blockade of Syracuse. Despite several setbacks, the Athenian naval leaders were still confident of victory. They did not know, however, that Alcibiades had betrayed them. When military forces led by the Spartan general Gylippus arrived to defend Syracuse, the Athenian fleet was caught off guard. The navy's chances of winning were further undermined when Lymarchus was killed. With both Lymarchus and Alcibiades gone, the Athenian navy was nearly powerless.

The situation was made even more dismal by the soldiers' poor living conditions. Having found no high ground for their camps, the Athenians had to settle in a swampy area where they were stricken with fever and various illnesses. Nicias—now the chief naval leader—had also fallen ill. By the summer of 413 B.C., all hope of victory had vanished.

Defeated by superstition

In an effort to strengthen the ailing campaign, Athens sent reinforcements under the command of General Demosthenes (384 B.C.–322 B.C.). Upon reaching the Athenian camp, however, he immediately realized that his forces were insufficient and he called for a retreat. Demosthenes probably would have been able to carry out the withdrawal if it had not been for

After being accused of vandalizing religious shrines, Alcibiades betrayed his former Athenian allies and created an alliance with Spartan king Agis II.

Nicias. Even though Nicias was sick and confined to his bed, he still had the power to keep the Athenian fleet from abandoning its mission. He foolishly believed that Syracuse might eventually surrender, so he ordered Demosthenes and his troops to stay. When the Athenians heard that more reinforcements were arriving for the Syracuse side, Demosthenes was finally able to get Nicias to agree to a retreat.

The Athenian navy would finally have retreated if Nicias had not intervened a second time. According to Thucydides (a Greek historian of Athens), Nicias was highly superstitious and believed in omens (premonitions or signs). When there was an eclipse of the full moon just as the Athenians were preparing to withdraw, Nicias issued an order that they stay. He believed the eclipse foretold disaster. In order to appease the gods, Nicias claimed, the Athenian forces would have to wait for a period of

ALCIBIADES Alcibiades was born into a wealthy family in Athens, Greece, in 450 B.C. His father, an Athenian army commander, was killed in 446 B.C at Coronea, Boetia, in central Greece. Unfortunately, this left the young Alcibiades without a stabilizing influence in his life. His guardian, the statesman Pericles (495 B.C.–429 B.C.), was too busy with politics to nurture the boy. When Alcibiades was older he became a pupil of Socrates (469 B.C.–399 B.C.). In his studies with Socrates, Alcibiades was impressed with the Athenian philosopher's idealism. By the time Alcibiades was thirty years old, however, he became greedy for political power and turned against his tutor.

After proving himself as a brave soldier and a brilliant speaker, Alcibiades was involved in peace negotiations between Athens and Sparta. When he rose to the rank of general in 420 B.C., he opposed the statesman Nicias, who had reached a peace agreement with Sparta. Alcibiades then formed an anti-Spartan alliance between Athens and the cities of Argos, Elis, and Matineia. The alliance was defeated in the Battle of Matineia (418 B.C.). To avoid ostracism, Alcibiades then joined forces with Nicias. In 415 B.C. he began the disastrous naval expedition against Syracuse.

time before moving out. Nicias's actions cost Athens the war.

Fleet is obliterated

The great naval expedition, which had begun with strong leadership, had become guided by superstition. While Nicias was waiting for the supposed hex (or spell) to run out, the Spartan commander Gylippus was mounting forces against him. Gylippus cut off the only Athenian escape route by blockading the harbor with Spartan ships. As a result, the only option for the trapped soldiers was to retreat onto the mainland. The waiting Syracusans and the Spartans then proceeded to obliterate the entire fleet. After killing both Nicias and Demosthenes, the Spartans took 7,000 prisoners. Virtually none of the 50,000 soldiers originally sent on the expedition returned to Athens. This terrible misadventure marked the end of Athens as a supreme naval power.

Alcibiades murdered

In 413 B.C., after seeking refuge in Sparta, Alcibiades fell out of favor with Agis II. He then fled to Persia, where he was given protection by the satrap (ruler) Tissaphernes. After the fall of the Spartan oligarchy called the "Four Hundred" in Athens two years later, Alcibiades was called back to command the Athenian fleet. He led the navy in a brief resurgence of its former glory by defeating the Peloponnesians off Cyzicus (a peninsula in present-day Turkey) in 410 B.C.

Alcibiades went on to recapture Byzantium (a city in ancient Thrace; now Istanbul, Turkey) in 408 B.C. Welcomed back to Athens as a hero the following year, he took control of the war. But Alcibiades's success was short-lived. In 406 B.C. the Spartan general Lysander defeated the Athenian fleet at Notium in Asia Minor, and Alcibiades was exiled to his castle on the Hellespont (now the Dardanelles, a narrow strait, or waterway, between Europe and Turkey).

Although now far removed from Athens, Alcibiades tried to influence the war—he once warned the Athenians about a surprise Spartan attack—but his advice was ignored. In 404 B.C. the Persian satrap Pharnbazus had Alcibiades murdered on orders from Lysander. That same year Lysander took over Athens, installing an oligarchy called the "Thirty Tyrants." The Peloponnesian War had come to a close, and the Spartans ruled the ancient world for the next three decades.

FOR FURTHER REFERENCE

Books

Ellis, Walter M. *Alcibiades*. New York City: Routledge, 1989.

Alexander in the Gedrosia Desert

325 B.C.

Alexander's ill-advised journey through Gedrosia led to the deaths of 60,000 people.

Alexander of Macedonia (also known as "Alexander the Great") was one of the most brilliant military leaders of all time. He was also one of the most charismatic figures in ancient history. Alexander is credited with spreading Hellenism (classical Greek ideals and values) throughout the civilized world. When he died at age thirty-three, Alexander ruled an immense empire that spanned more than 3,000 miles, from the Balkan Peninsula (in southeast Europe) to the Indus River (in present-day Pakistan).

As Alexander gained power, however, he became increasingly dictatorial in his relationships with his subjects and his troops. After a grueling seven-year campaign to conquer the Persian Empire, Alexander's soldiers finally revolted and forced their leader to go back to Macedonia. On the way back Alexander led a disastrous march across the Gedrosia desert which resulted in the loss of nearly 60,000 lives. By the time Alexander returned home, the Macedonians and Greeks had become thoroughly distressed by the young leader's behavior. During a celebratory banquet Alexander drank a cup of wine and immediately fell ill. He died twelve days later. The cause of Alexander's death has remained open to question: Did he die of natural causes, or was he murdered?

Alexander the Great became king of Macedonia after the death of his father, King Philip II.

Sets out to conquer the Persians

After Alexander became king of Macedonia upon the death of his father, Philip II, in 334 B.C., he subdued all the remaining Greek city-states. (A city-state was an independent political unit that consisted of a city and the surrounding countryside.) Alexander then set out to complete his father's goal of conquering the Persian Empire. The campaign, which would last for seven years, was filled with victorious conquests. Alexander's army crossed the Hellespont (a narrow strait between Europe and Turkey now called the Dardanelles) and met the Persians in battle for the first time on the Granicus River (at the Sea of Mamara in Turkey). The Macedonian forces smashed the opposing army, although Alexander himself narrowly missed being killed.

Following this victory Alexander pressed on through Asia Minor into Turkey, where he met the army of the newly crowned King Darius III (550 B.C.–486 B.C.) of Persia. Cutting the Persians off as they retreated to the sea, Alexander's men inflicted a crushing defeat that left an enormous number of Persians dead.

As Darius fled to safety, Alexander was in hot pursuit, crushing the Persian fleet at its bases on the Mediterranean Sea. He then chased Darius to the Phoenician city of Tyre on an island off the coast of Lebanon. During the final battle in July 332 B.C., 8,000 Phoenicians were reportedly killed and 30,000 were taken as slaves. Before the devastation had ended, Alexander received a peace offer from Darius. The terms were so favorable that Alexander's second in command, Parmenion, reportedly said he would accept the offer if he were Alexander. "That," Alexander reportedly replied, "is what I should do were I Parmenion."

Proclaimed son of Amon-Ra

Still in pursuit of Darius, Alexander's army swept south, conquering all of Syria and crossing into Egypt. The Egyptians welcomed Alexander as a liberator from the hated Persians. They also proclaimed him the son of Amon-Ra, the supreme Egyptian deity (god). Historians speculate this may be one reason Alexander considered himself divine. The following winter he founded Alexandria, the largest of the seventy cities he established during the course of his conquest.

While in Egypt, Alexander visited the ancient oracle (a site where priests or priestess predicted the future) of Siwa (an oasis in northwest Egypt). Although Alexander did not reveal the oracle's prophecy, his soldiers spread the rumor that Alexander was said to be destined to rule the world. Early in 331 B.C. Alexander returned to Syria with an army of 400,000 foot soldiers and 7,000 cavalry (horse soldiers). Meeting Darius in Mesopotamia, he drove the Persian king into the city of Persepolis. Alexander burned palaces and ransacked the city, declaring himself the conqueror of the Persians. The Persian Empire would not entirely fall, however, for another three years.

Pursues Darius

Still in pursuit of Darius, Alexander approached Bactria (an ancient country in southwest Asia) where he learned that the king had been captured by Bessus, a cousin of Darius and the ruler of Bactria. After Bessus executed Darius, Alexander had the body taken back to Persepolis to be buried in the royal tombs. Now that the king of Persia was dead, Alexander adopted the title "Lord of Asia," the name given the ruler of the Persian Empire.

Alexander then learned that Bessus was also calling himself king and leading a revolt in the eastern provinces of the empire. Alexander marched his army across the Hindu Kush (a great mountain range in present-day Afghanistan) into Bactria, only to discover that Bessus had devastated the countryside and fled over the Oxus River (now known as the Amu Darya). By the time the Macedonian army overtook Bessus, he had already been removed from power. Alexander had Bessus formally tried for the murder of Darius and then had his nose and ears cut off before having him publicly put to death by crucifixion.

Alienates his soldiers

By this time Alexander's behavior had become increasingly despotic (oppressive), and his men were beginning to show their dissatisfaction. Alexander killed his own foster brother, Clitus, in a drunken brawl after Clitus insulted him. Alexander then antagonized his Greek and Macedonian followers by marrying a Bactrian princess named Roxana and adopting Persian manners and dress. In 330 B.C. Alexander learned of a conspiracy to murder him. Discovering that the son of his general Parmenion was implicated, Alexander not only had the son put to death, but he also executed Parmenion (who was innocent).

Alexander further alienated his soldiers by his treatment of the historian Callisthenes, a nephew of Aristotle, who had joined Alexander's expedition as official historian. At first Callisthenes portrayed Alexander as a godlike figure in his reports, but he became more and more critical of his leader's Persian garb and despotic behavior. Charging Callisthenes with being involved in the conspiracy against him, Alexander ordered the historian's execution.

Soldiers revolt

In 327 B.C. Alexander went back over the Hindu Kush into India. The following year he scaled Mount Aornos (now called Pir-Sar), a supposedly unconquerable summit. In the spring Alexander's army marched into the city of Taxila in India, where they were well received by the local princes. Alexander's men conquered the Indus Valley after defeating the army of King Porus on the Hydaspes River (the present-day Jhelum). This was, however, to be Alexander's last great battle. As he pushed east to the Hyphasis River (now called the Beas), his troops rebelled and refused to go any farther. They were tired of seven years of fighting, and they wanted to return to their families. Unable to persuade the men to press on, Alexander sulked for two days before agreeing to lead the army back home. In determining the best route for the return trip to the Mediterranean, Alexander decided to test the prevailing theory that the Indus and the Nile were one river.

Alexander constructed a large fleet of boats for sending part of his army downstream on the Jhelum to the Indus delta. He divided the remainder of his forces into three groups that would make the journey by land. Departing down the river in November 326 B.C., Alexander engaged in constant warfare because the Indians would not provide supplies to his troops without a fight. According to one account, at the modern-day

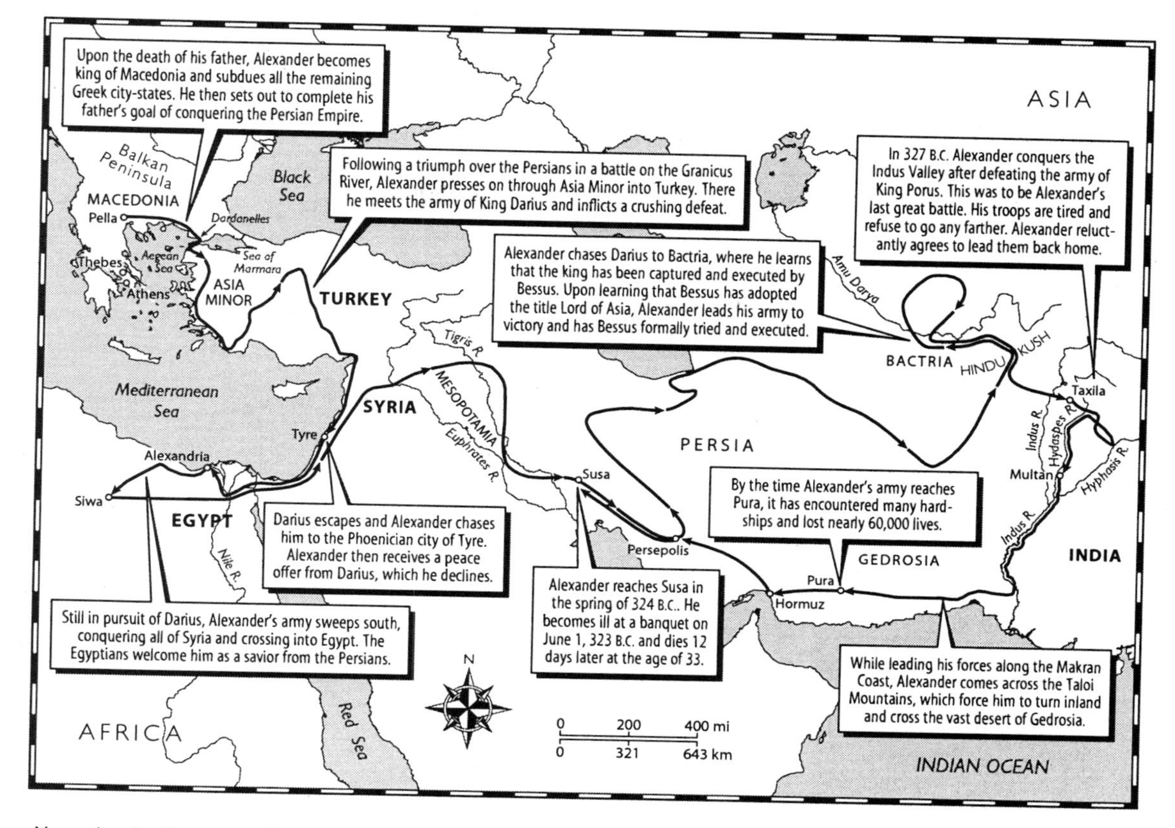

Alexander the Great was obsessed with expanding his empire. Over the course of its travels, Alexander's army explored lands in the Balkans, India, Egypt, and Iran.

city of Multan, Alexander climbed a ladder to lead an attack and was badly wounded. For several days, as he appeared to be near death, his men went berserk, destroying the city and killing its inhabitants. When Alexander recovered from his wounds, he continued the journey down the river. Upon reaching the Indus delta in the summer of 325 B.C., he determined the river was not connected to the Nile.

Heads back to Macedonia

Before the expedition reached the Indian Ocean, Alexander sent Craterus, one of his senior officers, back to Persia with the largest part of the army. He then instructed another of his officers, a man named Nearchus, to wait until the monsoon (storm) season in October before sailing along the coast to the Persian Gulf. From there Nearchus was to find a sea route back to the mouth of the Euphrates River in eastern Turkey. The object was to open a trade route from the Euphrates to the Indus.

Meanwhile, Alexander and the remainder of his forces would make their way on land along the unexplored Makran coast (now part of Pakistan), where he intended to build supply depots for the ships. But the Taloi Mountains, which extend all the way to the coast, forced Alexander to turn inland. Since the mountains presented such a forbidding obstacle, Alexander had no alternative but to lead his party across a vast expanse of desert in Gedrosia (now part of Pakistan and Iran). This journey, which lasted from August to October in 325 B.C., was the most difficult trek of Alexander's campaign.

Leads disastrous Gedrosia crossing

Alexander's army maintained a route near the coast of the Indian Ocean for as long as possible. At the beginning of their journey they came upon an unfriendly tribe called the "Fish-Eaters." The tribesmen had hairy bodies, long tangled hair, and claw-like fingernails. Their clothes were made of animal hides or shark skin, and they lived in huts built from whale skeletons. Fish was a primary food source, and all of the Fish-Eaters' cattle ate fish meal; as a result, the tribe's butchered cattle meat had a fishy taste. No crops grew on the land, and Alexander's soldiers were unable to find much food.

Conditions grew even worse when the men had to go directly into the desert and began running out of water. Sending parties ahead to dig wells, Alexander traveled primarily at night to reduce the number of deaths from heat stroke. The wells, however, were twenty-five to seventy-five miles apart. By the time the soldiers reached water, they were literally dying of thirst. Historians cite accounts of men in full armor throwing themselves into the wells, then dying from over-drinking.

As the army advanced farther into the desert, the wagons sank into sand dunes and soldiers' boots filled with sand. Deadly snakes were a constant hazard, and poisonous plant life killed great numbers of animals and soldiers. Although edible dates grew on palm trees, the fruit was frequently unripe and choked people to death. Alexander had hoped to ration supplies, but by now his men were breaking into food cases and killing pack animals for meat. One night an even more devastating disaster struck the baggage train, which was camped in a dry valley area. A violent rainstorm rolled down from the hills, releasing a flood of water into the darkness and sweeping away tents, baggage, animals, and nearly all the women and children.

Thousands of lives lost

Having escaped the flood, Alexander's army was caught in a sandstorm that erased landmarks. Having no means of staying on course toward the coast, the party drifted farther into the desert. Recognizing the emergency, Alexander took a small cavalry party and rode toward the sea. Upon reaching the Indian Ocean the group dug several wells and struck fresh water. When the army finally rejoined Alexander's smaller party, they proceeded along the coast for a week, striking a plentiful supply of water. At last Alexander's guides found the road that led to Pura, the capital of Gedrosia.

Marching into the city sixty days after he had set out across the desert, Alexander calculated his losses. They were astounding. When the expedition started out, Alexander's forces totaled about 85,000 people, most of them noncombatants (nonmilitary personnel). There were now no more than 25,000 people remaining. Cavalry troops, who had originally numbered 1,700 men, were reduced to 1,000. All the horses, pack mules, supplies, and equipment were gone. It was another four months before Alexander and Nearchus met at the port of Hormuz on the Persian Gulf.

Followers alarmed

Alexander's army reached Susa (an ancient city in present-day Iran) in the spring of 324 B.C. By this time the young leader's men had become even more distressed by his behavior. Alexander had taken another wife and integrated Persians into his army. These measures so alarmed Greek and Macedonian veterans that they voiced their discontent. Alexander discharged these soldiers, and many set out for Europe.

After the Gedrosian disaster Alexander became more suspicious and irrational. He drank heavily, flew into rages, and increasingly took refuge in his own divinity. Yet Alexander also made plans for future expeditions. He sent one of his officers, Herclides, to explore the Caspian Sea and determine whether it

ALEXANDER THE GREAT

Alexander was born in 356 B.C. in Pella, Macedonia (or Macedon, an ancient kingdom lying near the Aegean Sea on the Balkan Peninsula). His father was King Philip II (382 B.C.–334 B.C.) and his mother was Olympias, Philip's first wife. Olympias strongly influenced Alexander by introducing him to mysticism (belief in direct communication with God) and art. Another important figure in Alexander's early life was his tutor, the Athenian philosopher Aristotle (384 B.C.–322 B.C.), who gave the boy a classical education. As Alexander was growing up, Philip expanded the Macedonian kingdom to include the neighboring Greek city-states of Thrace, Chalcidice, Thessaly, and Epirus. By the time Alexander was twelve years old, Philip had either conquered all the Greek city-states or forced them into an alliance. Philip was making plans to invade the Persian Empire when he was assassinated at the wedding of his daughter to the king of one of his vassal (conquered) states. According to unproven reports, Olympias (and possibly even Alexander) was involved in Philip's murder because the king had neglected Olympias in favor of his other wives.

Alexander succeeded to the throne at the age of nineteen. The unhappy Greeks revolted, but Alexander quickly put them down, demonstrating his genius as a military leader. He also subdued uprisings in Thrace and Illyria, two other countries on the Balkan Peninsula. When people in the Greek city of Thebes revolted on a false rumor that Alexander was dead, he moved in and destroyed everything but the temples and the house of Pindar, the famous Greek poet. Having subdued the whole of Greece, Alexander became intent on carrying out his father's plan to conquer the Persians. He headed east on a march that was to become one of the greatest military conquests in history.

connected to the ocean, which was thought to stretch across the world. Alexander was going to place Nearchus in command of a fleet that would sail around Arabia in search of a route between India and the Red Sea. He apparently intended to conquer Arabia as well. These projects were abandoned, however, when Alexander became ill at a banquet on June 1, 323 B.C. He died twelve days later at the age of thirty-three. Alexander's only son, Alexander IV (323 B.C.–310 B.C.), was born to Roxana after his death.

Was Alexander murdered?

Many historians have suggested that Alexander died of a fever, although observers at the time reported that he had been poisoned. Twentieth-century biographers tend to confirm the ancient theory, concluding that a dose of poison was mixed into Alexander's wine by enemies in his own ranks. Evidence shows that Alexander's lieutenants could no longer tolerate his tyranny. In addition to costing thousands of lives, the journey through Gedrosia had exacted a severe political—and personal—toll on the young king.

FOR FURTHER REFERENCE

Books

Wepman, Dennis. *Alexander the Great.* New York City: Chelsea House, 1986.

Wood, Michael. *In the Footsteps of Alexander the Great: A Journey from Greece to Asia.* Los Angeles: University of California Press, 1997.

Other

In the Footsteps of Alexander the Great. [Videocassette] Public Broadcasting Service (PBS-TV), 1998.

The Battle of Hattin

1187

After the Battle of Hattin, Christians did not regain full access to Jerusalem until the late nineteenth century.

The Battle of Hattin in 1187 was one of the most important events of the Middle Ages (a period between A.D.500 and A.D.1500). In a confrontation with Christian crusaders, the Muslim army recaptured the city of Jerusalem, the capital of the Holy Land, which had been seized by the Christians during the First Crusade in 1099. For the Christians, the battle was a disaster that could have been avoided. The failure was in large part due to the actions of Guy of Lusignan, the king of Jerusalem, who made significant errors in judgement. Preparing for a confrontation with the Muslims, Guy had pulled together all of his resources. He then marched his mighty army of crusaders into a trap set by the Muslim general Saladin. The resulting battle took place on a dry desert under the intense heat of the sun. These horrible conditions put the heavily armored Christian knights at a disadvantage against the Muslims, who were accustomed to the hot, dry climate. Guy's defeat at the Battle of Hattin resulted in the Christians having no access to Jerusalem and the Holy Land for the next 800 years.

Muslims seize Holy Land

The Holy Land (now known as Palestine) is a region comprised of parts of present-day Israel, Jordan, and Egypt. The area is considered sacred by Jews, Muslims, and Christians.

Jerusalem (also called Zion; the capital of modern Israel) is regarded as the "holy city" and the center of the Holy Land by these three religions. Jews and Christians in particular revere Jerusalem as the capital of the Messiah (the expected king who will deliver the Jews).

The significance of the Battle of Hattin must be traced back to the seventh century, when the Egyptian caliph Umar (c. 581–644) captured Jerusalem, the capital of the Holy Land. (A caliph is a Muslim leader considered to be the successor of Muhammed, the founder of Islam.) At first the Muslims permitted Christians to continue pilgrimages (trips to a sacred place) to Jerusalem, but in the eleventh century the caliph Hakim (966-1021) started persecuting Christian worshippers. In 1071 Jerusalem fell under the control of the more ruthless Selijuk (Muslim) Turks. This event gave rise to the Crusades, a series of wars waged by Christians to recapture Jerusalem, from 1095 to 1291.

The First Crusade

After Jerusalem fell to the Turks, Pope Urban II (c. 1042-1099; head of the Roman Catholic Church) declared war on the Muslims. At the Council of Clermont (a church meeting held in France in 1095), he rallied Christians and organized the First Crusade to reclaim the Holy Sepulcher (the tomb of Christ). Urban issued crosses to the Christian soldiers, who were called "crusaders" (after the word "crux," the Latin term for cross). Urban urged the men on with the battle cry "Deus volt!" ("God wills it!"), pronouncing the crusade a holy mission that would count as full penance (forgiveness from sin) for all participants.

As wandering preachers carried news about the crusade, the movement spread throughout Europe and into Scandinavia. Soon hordes of volunteers joined the Christian army. The First Crusade was a success. In 1099 the Christians retook Jerusalem and established the Latin Kingdom of Jerusalem. By 1140 the crusaders had expanded their territory in the Holy Land along the entire eastern coast of the Mediterranean Sea. Crusader states included the Kingdom of Armenia, the County of Edessa, the Principality of Antioch, the County of Tripoli, and the island of Cyprus. Within seven years, however, Edessa had fallen to the Turks.

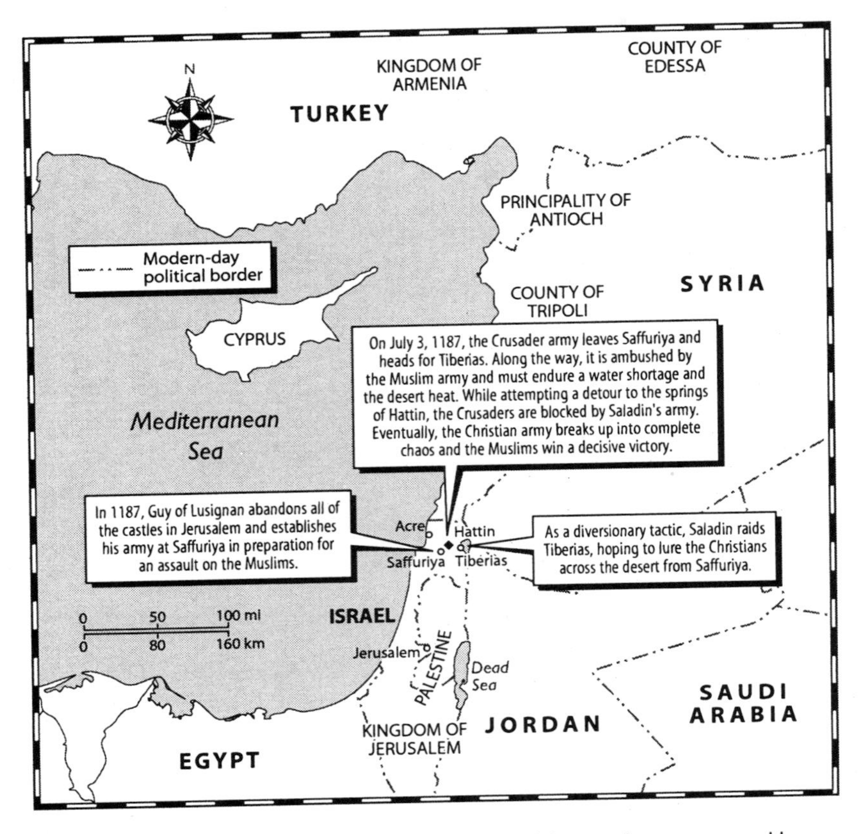

The crusader soldiers were both ill-equipped for desert fighting and outmaneuvered by Saladin's forces. As a result, the Christian army lost many men to injury and desertion.

Latin Kingdom of Jerusalem weakened

By 1187 the Latin Kingdom of Jerusalem had become divided and weak, having been split into two political factions. On one side were the native lords—all descendants of the First Crusaders—led by Raymond of Tripoli (1140–1187). On the other side were the "new men," or recent arrivals to the kingdom. Among these men was the king of Jerusalem, Guy of Lusignan. Other important groups were the Hospitallers and the Templars, military orders that had been established in the kingdom at that time. Hospitaller and Templar knights were not particularly loyal to either faction. Nonetheless, the leader of the Templars, a man named Gerard of Ridefort, hated Raymond of Tripoli, so that the situation became ripe for treachery. (Gerard had been instrumental in bringing Guy into power over the kingdom.)

At the same time the Christian stronghold was falling apart, the rival Muslims were becoming stronger. They had become united under a single ruler named Saladin (1138–1193), with the sole purpose of taking back Jerusalem from the crusaders. Saladin was anxious to exploit the weakness of the Christians. He knew they were divided and that Guy was a poor leader. Saladin also realized, however, that as long as the crusaders continued to occupy the kingdom, they would become stronger. In order to be victorious, Saladin needed to draw the Christians out of their castles and into the wide-open desert where they would be exposed to the hot sun. He could attack the kingdom.

At the time of the Battle of Hattin, the Muslims had become united under Saladin's rule. Saladin understood the crusaders' weak spots and targeted them in battle.

Saladin sets trap

In 1187 Guy had abandoned all of the castles in Jerusalem and established his army at Saffuriya in preparation for an assault on the Muslims. Now that the Christians were vulnerable, Saladin decided to set a trap for them. First he used a diversionary tactic by raiding Tiberias (a city on the Sea of Galilee in Israel). Saladin knew that Raymond of Tripoli, a commander in the royal army, was also in Saffuriya, but his wife was in Tiberias. Saladin predicted that Guy would want to retreat to Tiberias in order to rescue Raymond's wife. As part of his strategy, Saladin hid troops along the passage between Saffuriya and Tiberias, then waited for Guy to fall for his trick. Since this area was a waterless desert, Saladin was certain that battle would be difficult for the royal army.

After receiving news about the situation at Tiberias, Guy did not immediately turn around and run back. Instead, he called a war council in order to hear the advice of his senior officers. Raymond of Tripoli surprisingly argued against returning to Tiberias to rescue his wife. In fact, he presented a strong argument for not embarking on the campaign. First, he bargained that Saladin was an honorable man who would not harm his wife. Raymond also warned that Saladin was planning an ambush. He pointed out that the passage between Saffuriya and Tiberias was a waterless desert region where the entire royal army could be lost in one small battle.

Crusaders ill-equipped

Almost everyone in the royal army was initially convinced by Raymond's argument, including King Guy. Gerard of Ridefort, however, stepped forward and called Guy a coward for allowing Tiberias to be sacked. Later, Gerard confronted the impressionable Guy and convinced him to change his mind about the campaign. At last Guy decided to go against Raymond's wise counsel and to march back to Tiberias. The royal army was shocked by this turn of events because they knew they could not win a battle in the desert.

The crusader army left Saffuriya early in the morning on July 3, 1187. The army was comprised of 15,000 soldiers, with 1,500 knights in full armor. Raymond of Tripoli led the procession out of Saffuriya to begin the fifteen-mile march to Tiberias. Along the way, just as Saladin had planned, the crusaders encountered the Muslim army (also referred to as the Saracens). Even though the Muslims were a major threat, the crusaders had to contend with two even greater dangers—a shortage of water and the desert heat. Wearing full armor in the middle of the desert was unbearable. Each soldier carried his own water bottle, but the supply quickly ran out.

The attack begins

By mid-morning, the sun was high in the sky, and the crusaders were under full attack by Saladin's army. At first, the crusaders managed to hold off the assault, but the lack of water and the hot sun were slowing them down. In spite of the terrible conditions, Guy commanded his men to continue marching toward Tiberias. Then Raymond of Tripoli suggested detouring to the springs of Hattin for water, and Guy agreed. As soon as the crusaders changed direction, however, Saladin's army was there to meet them, blocking their path to Hattin. Raymond of Tripoli wanted to engage the enemy immediately, but Guy issued an order to halt the march and set up camp instead. This was a major mistake, for the crusaders had to spend the night in the desert with no water while being terrorized by the Saracens.

GUY OF LUSIGNAN Guy of Lusignan (c. 1129–1194) was born into the prominent Lusignan family of western France. He came from a line of Christian crusaders that began with Hugh I in the tenth century. Guy's father, Hugh VIII, also had two other, more successful sons. The eldest son, Hugh IX, was Hugh VIII's successor. Hugh IX was the father of Hugh X, who was instrumental in a revolt against King Henry III of England. Guy's other brother, Amalric (d. 1205), was the powerful king of Cyprus. Guy became the king of Jerusalem in 1186 by marrying Sibyl, the sister of King Baldwin IV.

When the crusaders started out again the next morning, morale was very low. Having lost their horses, many of the knights were now marching with the infantry (foot soldiers). Some of the men were so frustrated that they defected to the Muslims. As the day wore on, the sun got hotter and the crusaders became thirstier. Finally, in an act of total desperation, the infantry abandoned their ranks and ran for the hills, where they thought water could be found. Yet Saladin's army was still blocking the entrance to Hattin. Finally, because of low morale, intense heat, and Saracen attacks, the Christian advance broke up into complete chaos.

Muslims recapture their kingdom

In response to the disintegration of his forces, Guy once again halted the march. He then set up the royal tent and rallied his troops. This was Guy's last mistake. The Saracens proceeded to attack and loot the tent. In a final sweep, they stole an important holy relic (or artifact): The True Cross from the Bishop of Lydda (or Lod, a Christian area in central Israel). The True Cross was considered the symbol of God's support of the Christians in battle. Without the cross, the morale of the crusader soldiers collapsed completely and the battle was over. Guy himself was so defeated that he simply sat down and waited to be captured as Saladin's army took the crusaders prisoners. Only Raymond of Tripoli and Balian of Ibelin managed to escape.

The Battle of Hattin was a decisive victory for the Muslims. As the result of a single maneuver, they managed to recapture their entire kingdom. Guy made several mistakes that contributed to this defeat. Since Guy had stripped all of his castles in order to gather resources for a campaign against the Muslims, the Saracens had no problem capturing almost every city in the Christian kingdom. Most crucially, he had allowed his army to fall into a trap in spite of warnings from his own officers. Once he made the decision to return to Tiberias, Guy doomed his men to fighting in the hot desert against seasoned Muslim warriors. Finally, he had halted his army twice, thus making them an easy target for Saladin's troops.

Crusades a failure

Guy's misadventure foreshadowed the ultimate fate of the Crusades. Although seven more Crusades took place over the next 100 years, they all ended in disaster. Crusade leaders used poor military tactics and fought among themselves. Many of the crusaders were also motivated by profit rather than a sense of religious duty. One of the most tragic Crusades was the Children's Crusade (see "Exploration and Adventure" entry), which was led by French peasant Stephen of Cloyes in 1212. Doomed to failure after the fall of Hattin, the crusaders lost their last stronghold at Acre (a seaport city in Israel) in 1291. Christians did not regain full access to Jerusalem and the Holy Land until the late nineteenth century.

FOR FURTHER REFERENCE

Books

Biel, Timothy L. *The Crusades*. San Diego, CA: Lucent Books, 1995.

The English Expedition to Cádiz

1625

The incident that finally destroyed the expedition was a drunken riot among English soldiers after they entered the Spanish town.

During the sixteenth century England had the most powerful navy in the world. In 1588, for example, English admirals performed brilliantly in their legendary defeat of the Spanish Armada. By the early 1600s, however, England no longer ruled the seas. In 1625 the English expedition to Cádiz, Spain, demonstrated how far the navy's reputation—and readiness—had fallen. Commanders, troops, and ships were not fit for the mission to capture Cádiz, a city that was becoming a major center for Spanish trade with the American colonies. Many factors played a role in the expedition's failure, from bad weather to a lack of food and clothing for the ships' crews. Perhaps the greatest obstacle facing the mission's success, however, was the disobedience and laziness of the crewmen. In fact, the incident that finally destroyed the expedition was a drunken riot among English soldiers after they entered the Spanish town.

Inadequate crews and equipment

The original commander of the Cádiz expedition was Lord High Admiral George Villiers, first Duke of Buckingham (1592–1628), a man who knew little about the sea. Before handing over the command to a more competent military man named Edward Cecil (1572–1638), Buckingham appointed his friends

The original commander of the Cádiz expedition was Lord High Admiral George Villiers, first Duke of Buckingham.

and relatives to all the other important positions. Six of the senior commanders had no warfare experience. The army of 10,000 men was largely made up of social misfits who lacked proper clothes, food, and training.

The fleet's condition matched the incompetence of its crews. Ninety vessels were assembled, including nine king's ships that were supposedly well equipped with artillery, thirty armed merchantmen (commercial vessels), and Newcastle colliers (ships carrying coal). England's Dutch allies also supplied fifteen ships. Although the fleet might have appeared impressive, many of the ships were being reused after serving in the Spanish Armada. Most of the vessels were old and slow, with damaged and torn sails.

Problems arose before the expedition even set sail. The soldiers, who were supposed to be getting weapons training in the countryside, had no money for food. They therefore took matters into their own hands and ran through the countryside, killing sheep and threatening anyone who got in their way. Because of the soldiers' behavior, their weapons were taken away, consequently leaving them with no training.

Incompetent recruits

As the senior officers surveyed their recruits, they found that the soldiers' dismal appearance matched their incompetence. Out of 2,500 men, 200 were physically inept, 24 were seriously ill, 26 were over the age of 60, and 4 men were blind. Also in the group were a minister, a madman, and many men who had deformities. One man had no toes and another man had one leg nine inches shorter than the other. Many rich, capable men had paid a fee so that they would not have to serve on the expedition; as a result, only the poor and infirm were left to take on the task.

Despite the sad state of the army and the fleet, the expedition set sail from Plymouth, on the southwest coast of England, on October 8, 1625. From the start, one ship was leaking so

THE SPANISH ARMADA The legendary English defeat of the Spanish Armada took place in 1588 at the height of England's rule of the seas. The Armada was a fleet of swift, powerful ships launched by Philip II (1527–1598) of Spain to invade England. The Catholic king planned to overthrow the Protestant queen Elizabeth I (1533–1603) and place himself on the English throne. The Spanish began organizing the invasion in 1586, but the following year British admiral Francis Drake staged a surprise attack on the Spanish fleet.

When the Armada finally set sail from Lisbon, Portugal (a port on the Atlantic Ocean), in May 1588, it consisted of 130 transport and merchant ships carrying 30,000 men. The fleet was on its way to Flanders (a country that is now part of Belgium) to pick up the army of the duke of Parma (now Emilia Romagna, a province in northern Italy). During the voyage the Armada was forced to stop at a seaport on the southwest coast of Spain by a storm. The fleet set out again in July, but failed to connect with Parma.

By the time the Armada was approaching the English Channel (a waterway between England and France), English ships had left Plymouth (on the southwest coast of England) and were sailing through the Channel toward the Spanish fleet. The English managed to attack the Armada four times, but did not inflict any serious damage. On August 6, 1588, the Armada anchored off Calais (a seaport in northern France) near the eastern entrance to the Channel, to wait for Parma's army. Spanish commanders were under orders not to fight the English in the Channel until Parma's men arrived. The next night English fire ships moved into the middle of the Armada and sent the Spanish vessels scattering. On August 8 the English staged a direct attack.

The crippled Armada was unable to regroup, but the wind abruptly changed and carried the ships north toward safety. As the Spanish ships tried to sail home past Scotland, they became separated by a raging storm. Many vessels were forced to land on the west coast of Ireland, where Spanish crewmen were killed by English troops. Only about half of the Armada returned to Spain.

badly it had to return home. There were not enough provisions (food and other supplies) for the men, and soon violent storms broke out at sea. High winds sank many of the ships. *Anne Royal*, Cecil's flagship (lead vessel), was damaged when the cannons broke loose. The crew was only able to keep the ship afloat by constantly pumping out water.

Disaster and disobedience

After the weather cleared, Cecil called a meeting to assess the damage and to establish order among the crews. Immedi-

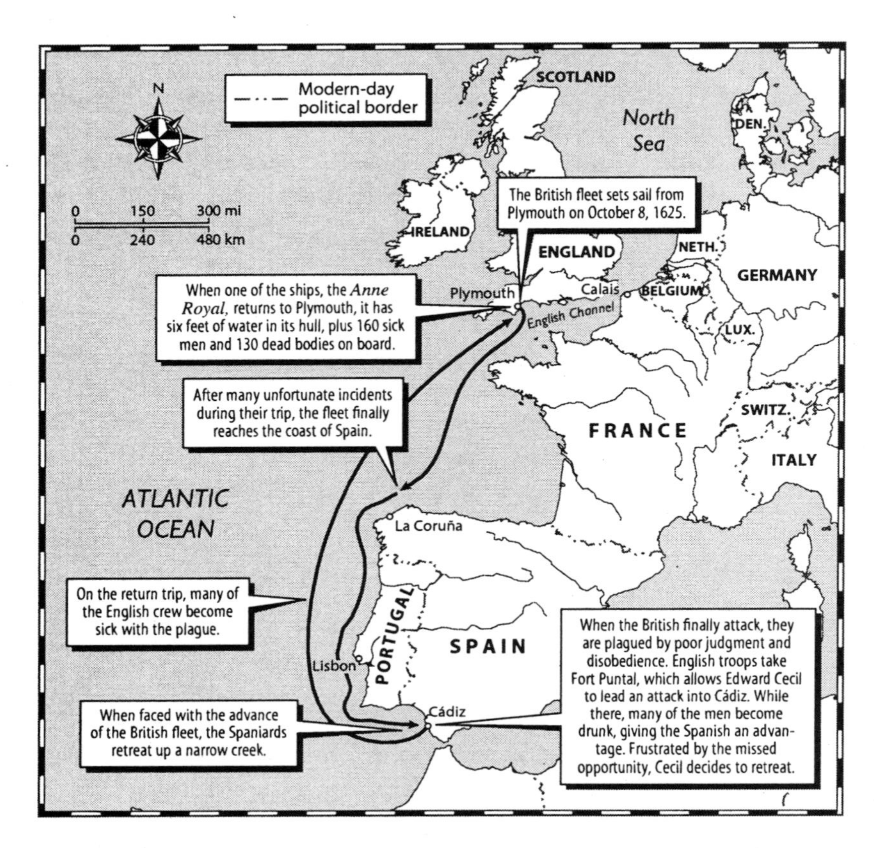

The British expedition to Cádiz was mismanaged and poorly manned from the start. In fact, most of the English troops were seriously ill, old, or physically inept.

ately his captains bombarded him with complaints. Cecil learned that the gunpowder and food were soaked, the water was no longer fit to drink, and many of the weapons were not working. Compounding these problems was the loss of contact with the squadron of forty ships under the command of Robert Devereux, the third Earl of Essex (1591–1646). As the English fleet approached the coast of Spain, lookouts (sailors who monitor the seas) then thought they sighted enemy ships. Cecil sent ships to chase the enemy away. The "enemy," however, turned out to be some of Essex's ships that had failed to identify themselves according to naval procedures. Essex's disobedient nature would turn out be a crucial hindrance to the entire expedition.

Essex's next violation came when he was ordered to find anchorage (locations for anchoring ships) off Cádiz Bay. Instead, he attacked twelve Spanish galleons (heavy ships) that were accompanied by fifteen galleys (boats propelled by oars). The rest of the English fleet had to bail Essex out of danger. When faced with the advance of the English fleet, the Spaniards retreated up a narrow creek. Finally achieving his first victory, Cecil had the Spaniards in a precarious spot. Because the English now had a dominant position, they thought they could destroy the Spanish ships whenever they felt like it.

Attack begins

Meanwhile, Cecil was given information that Cádiz was not strongly armed. In theory, the English could easily take the city in a sweeping attack. Cecil listened to his captains, however, who advised him to wait and stage an initial assault on Fort Puntal, which protected Cádiz in the bay. At sundown, twenty Newcastle colliers and five Dutch warships began the attack, while three English men-of-war (battleships) formed a second line of defense. Chaos erupted. The crews aboard the colliers disobeyed orders and remained anchored because their captains were unwilling to risk their ships. The Dutch then tackled the fort alone.

Because they had no backup, the Dutch soldiers were severely injured and one of their ships was lost. When Essex stepped forward to help with the fighting, the colliers still hung back. After the ships finally began firing, they hit the stern (rear end) of the *Anne Royal*. Although the English shot over 2,000 rounds of ammunition, they inflicted very little damage on Puntal. At long last, after a twenty-four-hour-siege, the English took the fort. During this time, however, the Spanish had been able to bring reinforcements to Cádiz from nearby military posts.

Troops get drunk

Upon hearing news that Spanish troops had been spotted, Cecil led 8,000 men into the city to try to stop the advance. More mayhem was to follow. After the English soldiers had stopped for a rest, Cecil was alerted that many of the men had not brought any food and were starving. He had no choice but to send the men back. When night fell, the remaining men set up camp near some deserted buildings. When they discovered that wine was stored in the buildings, Cecil kindly allowed one butt (barrel) of wine for each regiment (a military unit consisting of several battalions, or two or more companies of soldiers). This gesture was a disastrous mistake. The men, who had not eaten and had been exposed to extreme heat, became drunk.

Before long, the scene became a drunken mess. The men broke into the wine supply, smashed open casks (barrels), and fired their weapons wildly into the air. They threatened each other and menaced any officer who tried to stop them. All forms of discipline were abandoned. When Cecil tried to have the wine taken away, the men dipped their helmets into it and drenched Cecil while threatening his life. For the rest of the night, the officers had to protect themselves from their own men.

Cecil retreats

The following morning Cecil had no choice but to return to Puntal, leaving drunk men scattered everywhere and vulnerable to attack by the Spanish. As the English soldiers marched out of Cádiz, men with hangovers abandoned their weapons and equipment along the road. The Spanish, in turn, took advantage of the episode by sinking four hulks (bodies of old, unused ships) across the entrance of the creek, thereby allowing only one English warship to enter at a time. Furious over the loss of such a great opportunity, Cecil concluded that he had no choice but to retreat.

Plague takes lives

The soldiers, however, were forced to spend one more night in the fields outside Cádiz. At this point nearly starving and unclothed, the men were pelted by storms and intense rain. Once the English were finally able to depart from Cádiz Bay, the trip home only became worse for the already fatigued troops. During the voyage a plague (an epidemic disease) broke out on some of the ships in the fleet. Many of the crewmen were so sick that they could not sail their ships. Cecil's solution was to send two healthy men to each of the ships in exchange for two sick men. As a result, the plague was spread from ship to ship.

The *Anne Royal* barely made it into port at Plymouth because six feet of water was standing in its hull (the body of a ship). Also aboard were 160 sick men and 130 dead bodies. Cecil and Essex went to the king's court to report to Buckingham on the Cádiz disaster. The two men then returned to comfortable lives. Most of the crew, however, spent their remaining days in poverty and sickness.

FOR FURTHER REFERENCE

Books

Martin, Colin, and Geoffrey Parker. *The Spanish Armada.* New York City: Norton, 1988.

Regan, Geoffrey. *The Book of Military Blunders.* Santa Barbara, CA: ABC-CLIO, 1991, pp. 142–45.

The Battle of Poltava

1709

The Swedish army lost the Battle of Poltava because of a squabble between two of its generals.

Throughout history important battles have been lost because allied generals could not get along. The defeat of the Swedish army at the Battle of Poltava in 1709 is an example of what happens when there is conflict within army ranks. King Charles XII of Sweden was a great military leader who had held the Russian city of Poltava under siege for three months. Problems arose, however, because his commanding officers, General Lewenhaupt and Field Marshal Count Karl Gustaf Rehnskold, hated each other. As a result, when Charles was injured and command was passed down to these two rivals, the siege of Poltava failed. In the end, Lewenhaupt was forced to surrender and the Russian army won the battle. Within twelve years, Sweden had also lost its status as a major military force in northern Europe.

Military machine breaks down

An eighteenth-century army was a complex organization. It was made up of several levels of officers and soldiers, including senior officers, junior officers, infantry (foot soldiers), and cavalry (soldiers on horseback). If any officer or soldier failed to do his duty, the entire military machine could break down. Such was the case when the Swedish blue coats (soldiers who wore blue coats) of Charles XII took on the Russian green coats (soldiers who wore green coats) of Peter the Great (1682–1725) at the Battle of Poltava in 1709.

The Swedish army had successfully invaded Russia in 1708. By mid-1709, however, as they camped outside Poltava (a city on the Vorskla River in the Ukraine), the Swedes had been weakened by long marches through extremely cold weather. The situation was made even worse because the Russian army greatly outnumbered the Swedish soldiers. Then a crisis occurred: Charles was seriously wounded in a skirmish and had to turn his command over to two of his subordinates, General Lewenhaupt and Field Marshal Count Karl Gustaf Rehnskold. Although Charles was an outstanding military commander, his strong leadership could not compensate for the weak bond between Lewenhaupt and Rehnskold.

Inferior leaders

Both Lewenhaupt and Rehnskold were fairly solid leaders, but certain circumstances began to take over at Poltava. For instance, Lewenhaupt experienced bouts of depression and paranoia. He believed that the whole world was plotting against him, including his own army. Rehnskold, on the other hand, had a strong temperament, yet he was worn out after years of battle. The poor living conditions in the Swedish camp outside Poltava had made Rehnskold restless and irritable. As a result, Rehnskold's poor disposition exaggerated Lewenhaupt's paranoia, which led to a growing hostility between the two men.

Rehnskold withholds plan

Whether or not Charles knew about these problems, he had no choice but to relinquish (or give up) his power. Since Rehnskold was a higher ranking officer than Lewenhaupt, he got to discuss battle plans with Charles directly. He talked secretly with the wounded king about how to attack a Russian camp that was stationed outside of Poltava. Charles may have assumed that Rehnskold would relay the plan to Lewenhaupt. The plan of attack, however, remained a secret between Rehnskold and the king. As a result, Lewenhaupt had limited information about the upcoming battle. All he knew was that he had to attack.

KING CHARLES XII Charles XII (1682–1718) began his reign as king of Sweden in 1697. An inexperienced youth of fifteen, he astounded his subjects when he crowned himself and dispensed with the traditional oath. In 1699 the neighboring countries of Russia, Poland, Saxony, and Denmark initiated the Northern War to take advantage of Charles's situation and topple Sweden, which then dominated northern Europe. The young king revealed his abilities as a military strategist, however, in a campaign that many scholars regard as one of the most brilliant in history. Between 1700 and 1707 the Swedish army, under Charles's leadership, defeated all of its enemy countries except Russia. In 1708 Charles moved into Russia against Peter I (also called Peter the Great) to clinch his final victory. The following year the two men's armies met outside the city of Poltava, where Charles was wounded and his forces were defeated.

Russians begin assault

Since Lewenhaupt had no idea what Rehnskold and Charles had planned, he was forced to mount an attack on his own. He advanced his infantry of 2,400 blue coats towards the Russian camp that contained 40,000 of Peter's soldiers. Even though Lewenhaupt was outnumbered, he managed to break through two Russian strongholds that were placed outside of the enemy camp. Then, just as Lewenhaupt was about to charge over the walls, he received a message from Rehnskold, telling him to retreat.

Lewenhaupt was furious at this turn of events, and the fragile bond between the two feuding commanders finally broke. Paranoia led the angry general to believe that Rehnskold was merely trying to prevent his moment of glory. Actually, the wise Rehnskold had decided to call off the battle because the blue coats were outnumbered. Despite this, Lewenhaupt defiantly ignored the message to retreat. Instead, he turned the infantry around and engaged the Russian ranks that he had just passed through. This act enraged Rehnskold, who confronted the delinquent commander on the battlefield and accused him of making a terrible mistake. Now that Lewenhaupt had turned his back on the Russian camp, green coats poured over the walls and advancing toward the Swedish troops. The Battle of Poltava had begun.

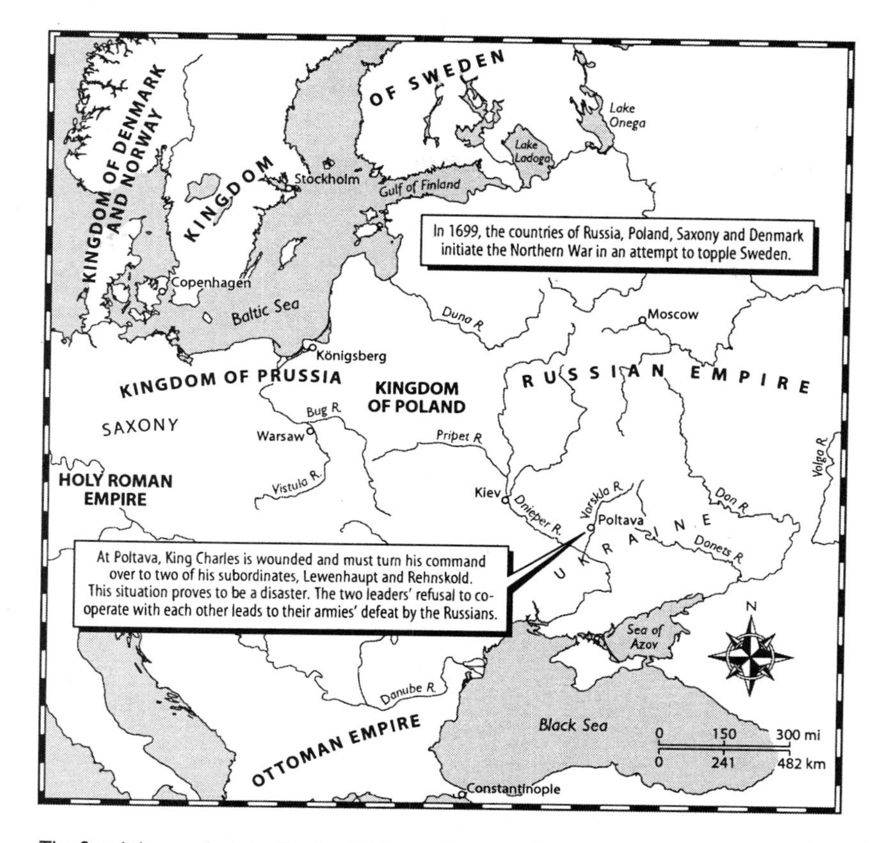

The Swedish army lost the Battle of Poltava when two of its generals could not get along on the battlefield.

Swedes defeated

Lewenhaupt and his troops were at a severe disadvantage because the Russians had cannons and the Swedes had only muskets (a type of gun similar to a rifle). Still, despite oncoming musket and cannon fire, Lewenhaupt broke through the first Russian line of attack. He even managed to seize a cannon and turn it against the green coats. After this small triumph, Lewenhaupt waited for the cavalry, led by Rehnskold, to sweep in and finish the job. Unfortunately, the cavalry was nowhere to be found. When Lewenhaupt turned to the left wing of his infantry, he found that the ranks had been decimated by Russian cannon fire. The edge that Lewenhaupt had achieved was quickly lost, and his blue coat army was scattered all over the battlefield. The failing general tried to rally his troops, but the Battle of Poltava was over and the Russians dominated.

Lewenhaupt retires to his bed

In the end, Lewenhaupt managed to escape with Charles, but the Russians took Rehnskold prisoner. The fact that his rival was finally out of the picture should have been refreshing news for Lewenhaupt, but he was just too exhausted to face the Russians. After the worn-out commander made it back to the Swedish base camp, he retired to his bed in the royal tent even though green coats were still advancing. Now that he was in his own camp, Lewenhaupt had an advantage over the Russians because he had more soldiers. Unfortunately, the physical and mental strain of battle had taken over and the defeated general was unfit for command. Lewenhaupt surrendered to the Russian army of Peter the Great on July 1, 1709.

Decline of Sweden

The defeat at Poltava marked the final stage of Sweden's decline as the foremost military power in northern Europe. After the battle, most of the Swedish soldiers were captured by Russia. Charles escaped to Turkey, however, and plotted a war between Russia and Turkey in 1710. When peace was declared the following year, the Turks asked Charles to leave their country. After he had resisted for nearly three years, an entire Turkish army set fire to his house and finally forced him out. By 1716 Charles had returned to Sweden. He later staged an invasion of Norway at Fredrikssten, where he was killed in battle. Charles's sister, Ulrica Leonora, succeeded him to the throne. During her reign, the Northern War came to an end and Sweden began to lose its military and political status.

FOR FURTHER REFERENCE

Books

Regan, Geoffrey. *The Book of Military Blunders*. Santa Barbara, CA: ABC-CLIO, 1991.

The Battle of Trenton

DECEMBER 26, 1776

The victory at Trenton was the spark George Washington needed to reinvigorate the American military effort.

The Battle of Trenton, which took place on December 26, 1776, was a turning point for the American colonies during the Revolutionary War. The battle marked the end of a losing streak for the American general George Washington and his troops. One of the decisive factors in the American victory was the negligence and overconfidence of the enemy commander, Johann Gottlieb Rall (died 1776). Rall underestimated the strength of the rebel army and was unprepared when it attacked. The Battle of Trenton has become one of the most popular stories in American history because of Washington's famous crossing of the Delaware River to take Rall and his troops by surprise.

Rall makes a big mistake

During the American Revolutionary War (1775–83; a war for American independence from Britain), Britain used a group of mercenaries (hired soldiers) called "Hessians" for military support. (Hessians are natives of the German state of Hesse.) The colonel of the Hessian army was Johann Gottlieb Rall, a boisterous, disrespectful, and overconfident leader. Rall was in charge of the Hessian troops who occupied the city of Trenton, New Jersey, in December 1776.

After Hessian commanders cancelled a dawn patrol, General George Washington and his men were able to stage a surprise attack at Trenton.

This was an important point in the war for both Britain and the American Continental Army, which was under the command of General George Washington. The previous month, British general William Howe (1729–1814) had captured Fort Washington on Manhattan Island (now part of New York City). The British had then forced the Americans to retreat through New Jersey across the Delaware River into Pennsylvania. Howe was retiring to his winter quarters, so he left Rall with the Hessian troops at Trenton.

For the most part, Rall was a man who wanted only to keep up appearances as a military commander. He drank too much, he gambled, and he was cruel to his men. Furthermore, he refused to show his true fear of the American rebels. For instance, when his officers warned him to fortify Trenton against attack, Rall merely brushed off the report. Rall hated the rebels, but it was a hatred that led him to disrespect them as soldiers. He claimed that the Hessians would not even have to fire their guns to defeat the weak rebel forces. Unfortunately for Britain, Rall was seriously mistaken.

Washington crosses the Delaware

Even though America was losing the war, soldiers in the Continental Army did not feel defeated. Washington, however, still needed a victory. He therefore decided to attack Trenton. In order to warn Rall, Washington sent the Hessian commander a message on Christmas day. Not surprisingly, Rall refused to read the letter because he was too busy celebrating. Meanwhile, Washington continued to advance his army of 2,400 troops. Since Rall had ignored the warning, none of his 1,400 mercenaries were aware of their impending doom.

At dawn on December 26, 1776, Washington and his men crossed the partially frozen Delaware River and took the

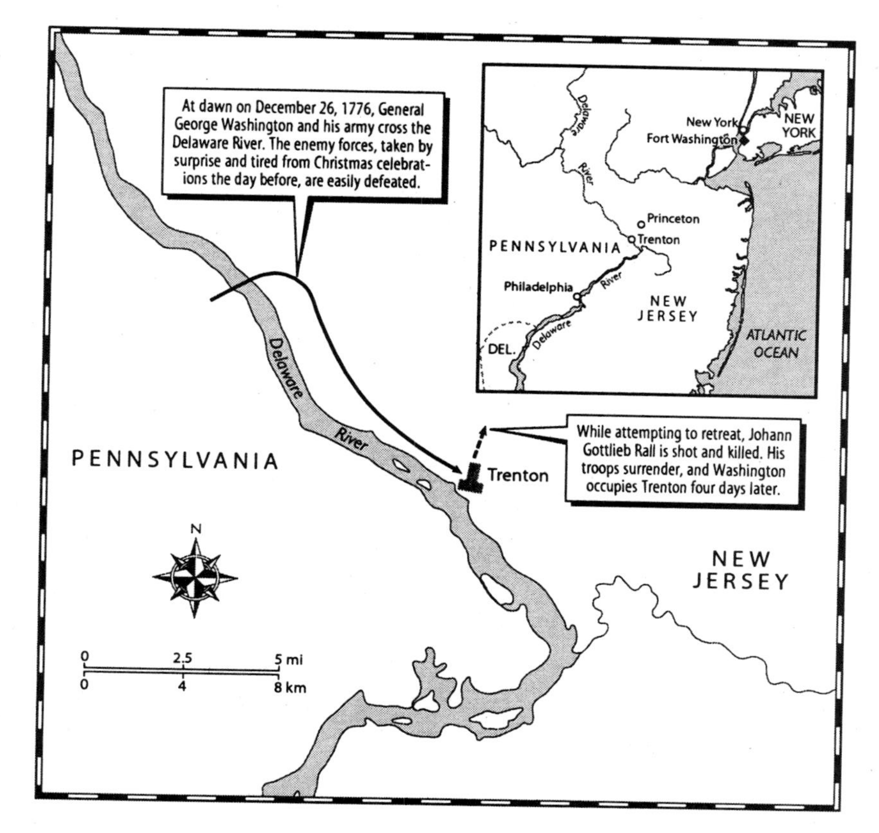

Hessian commander Johann Rall vastly underestimated the determination of rebel troops at the Battle of Trenton.

enemy forces at Trenton by surprise. Rall's army was unprepared because his second in command, Major von Dechow, had canceled the dawn patrol when the weather turned very cold. The rebels literally crept up behind the Hessians' backs and attacked. A Hessian officer immediately informed Rall, who was still in bed. The Hessians were slow to respond because they were still tired from their Christmas celebrations the night before.

Rall did manage a counterattack, but his soldiers were dominated by the Americans, who captured more than 900 men. Then, when the Hessians began to flee, Rall mounted his horse. Within seconds he was felled by a rebel bullet. Finally, just before he died, the defeated colonel managed to order his troops to surrender. Four days later Washington occupied Trenton.

GEORGE WASHINGTON

George Washington (1732–1799) was born in Westmoreland County, Virginia. As a young man he was a surveyor and participated in the westward expansion of the United States. Washington later fought in the French and Indian Wars (1689–63), during which he became a colonel. In 1759 Washington retired to Mount Vernon, his plantation in Virginia, and got married. In 1774 hostilities erupted with the British, leading to the American Revolution (1775–83).

In 1775, while Washington was a delegate in the Continental Congress (also known as the "Federal Legislature of the Thirteen American Colonies"), he was promoted to commander of the Continental forces. Washington's military campaign as a general began when he captured Boston, Massachusetts, from the British on May 17, 1776. Unfortunately, Washington suffered a brutal defeat when he lost New York City to occupation forces on August 27, 1776. After defeating the British at the Battle of Trenton on December 26, 1776, he spent a difficult winter at Valley Forge. Washington and his troops eventually rallied and scored a series of victories over the next five years, a successful run culminating in the surrender of British commander General Charles Cornwallis on October 19, 1781. Washington became president of the United States of America on April 30, 1789.

A force to be reckoned with

Suddenly, as a result of Rall's defeat at the Battle of Trenton, the Americans became a force to be reckoned with. The fact that they had taken the Hessians by surprise was proof that the rebels could not be dismissed as a threat by the enemy. Now, not only had Washington scored a decisive victory, but he had lost justfive soldiers in the skirmish. This was just the impetus he needed to reinvigorate the American military effort. On January 3, 1777, Washington and his men drove back the British at the Battle of Princeton and reestablished American control of New Jersey.

FOR FURTHER REFERENCE

Books

Fast, Howard. *The Crossing.* New York City: Morrow, 1971.

McPhillips, Martin. *The Battle of Trenton.* New York City: Silver Burdett, 1985.

Tecumseh's Campaign

MID-1790s TO 1813

"The annihilation of our race is at hand unless we unite in one common cause against the common foe."

—Tecumseh

Tecumseh was a Shawnee war chief and one of the most influential Native American leaders of his time. He envisioned an Indian confederacy that would enable native people to stand united against the threat posed by white settlement and territory expansion. Tecumseh spent much of his adult life campaigning among the tribes of the Old Northwest. Although he encountered many obstacles, he also won supporters for his cause. In the end, however, Tecumseh's great plan was defeated by the superior numbers and military technology of the white men. Differences of opinion among the tribes themselves also undermined the unity movement. Only a few decades after Tecumseh was killed at the Battle of the Thames, Indian lands fell entirely under the control of the U.S. government.

Tecumseh's early life

Tecumseh (c. 1768–1813) was born at Old Piqua, a Shawnee village on the Mad River in what is now western Ohio. (Tecumseh's name was probably originally pronounced "Tekamtha." The term "Tecumseh" can be translated as "Moves From One Place to Another," or "Shooting Star.") According to traditional native stories, a large meteor or comet passed through the sky at the moment of Tecumseh's birth, suggesting his name. Tecumseh's father, Puckeshinwa, was a respected

Shawnee war chief and his mother, Methoataske, was of Creek or possibly Cherokee origin. The family included at least four children in addition to Tecumseh. Chicksika was Tecumseh's oldest brother, and Tecumpease was an older sister. Two of Tecumseh's other brothers were named Sauwaseekau and Lalawethika.

Tecumseh displayed leadership qualities at an early age. He was a persuasive speaker, a skillful orator, and a brave fighter.

In 1774 Puckeshinwa was killed in a war between the Shawnee and the "Long Knives" (the Shawnee name for white settlers). Chicksika promised his dying father that he would teach young Tecumseh the skills of the hunter and warrior. At an early age Tecumseh displayed the leadership qualities that would mark his later career. He became famous for his abilities as a warrior and for his strong moral character. Historical accounts indicate that he married at least twice. He and his first wife, whose name is not known, apparently separated after a disagreement. Tecumseh's second wife, Mamate, died young and left him with a young son named Pachetha. The boy was raised by Tecumpease. Tecumseh may have had another son and perhaps a daughter with a Cherokee woman.

Gains fame as warrior

Tecumseh's abilities as a warrior were developed when he was a very young man. His first brush with battle seems to have been in 1782. At age fourteen he accompanied Chicksika, who was now a war chief, in an attack against a party of invading Kentuckians. Tecumseh soon made a name for himself as a brave and humane fighter. One time he reportedly objected to the burning of a white prisoner. He spoke so persuasively that his fellow warriors promised to abandon such practices in the future.

Tensions between the Shawnee and the Long Knives, however, continued to build. From 1787 to 1789 Chicksika's war party, which included Tecumseh, roamed the south, hunting and raiding white settlements. In 1788 Chicksika was killed in an abortive attack on Buchanan's Station in Tennessee. Most of the party returned home after the loss of their leader. Tecumseh, however, remained in the south for another two years.

"Mad" Anthony Wayne led an expedition against Native American forces at the Battle of Fallen Timbers in August 1792.

Northwest Territory created

While Tecumseh was traveling with the war party, the U.S. government created the Northwest Territory by taking many of the disputed Native American lands. (The Northwest Territory included the present states of Ohio, Indiana, Illinois, Michigan, Wisconsin, and part of Minnesota.) As the United States opened the region to white settlement, the government tried to put down Indian resistance with military action. The tribes decisively drove out expeditions led by General Josiah Marmar in 1790 and Arthur St. Clair (1736–1818), governor of the territory, in 1791. Tecumseh was home in time to lead the scouting party that kept the Indians informed of St. Clair's advance.

Following these defeats, the Americans took stronger measures. An expedition led by Major General "Mad" Anthony Wayne (1745–1796), the military commander of the west, clashed with the Indians at a place called Fallen Timbers in August 1792. The warriors were badly outnumbered and suffered a crushing defeat, which was made worse by the failure of promised aid from the British. Tecumseh was in the forefront of the fighting at Fallen Timbers, and his brother, Sauwauseekau, was among the men who were killed. Tecumseh took no part in the negotiations after the Battle of Fallen Timbers, which resulted in the Treaty of Greenville. As a result of the treaty, the Indians relinquished their claims to lands in southern, central, and eastern Ohio. Grieved by his brother's death and disappointed at the failure of British support, Tecumseh withdrew to western Ohio.

Has influence with Long Knives

The years following Fallen Timbers were relatively peaceful for Tecumseh. He lived with his followers for a time at Deer

Tecumseh's brother Lalawethika eventually adopted the name Tenskwatawa, or "The Open Door." In speeches to his people, Tenskwatawa urged a return to native traditions and a rejection of white men's ways.

Creek in western Ohio, then moved west to present-day Indiana. Tecumseh was instrumental in reconciling differences between the white settlers and Native Americans. Government officials often asked him to negotiate for them. On one such occasion frightened white settlers had abandoned their farms after Indian attacks. Tecumseh spoke calmly and eloquently to a group of whites, assuring them that the Indians intended to abide by the Treaty of Greenville and wanted to live in peace. Whites who heard Tecumseh's speech commented on his skills as an orator (public speaker), in spite of the fact that he always spoke in the Shawnee language and his words were translated by an interpreter.

Indian movement begins

In 1805 Tecumseh's younger brother, Lalawethika, initiated a religious revival that eventually became known as the "Indian Movement." Lalawethika attracted large numbers of followers from many tribes to a community he established on the site of present-day Greenville, Ohio. He urged a return to traditional Indian values and rejection of the ways of the white man. Perhaps most importantly, he emphasized that the whites had no right to the land they had taken from the Native Americans. Lalawethika then changed his name to Tenskwatawa ("The Open Door"; he was also known as the "Shawnee Prophet").

Tecumseh joined his brother at Greenville. Under Tecumseh's influence the movement turned in a political, rather than religious, direction. Tecumseh had two major goals: common ownership of all remaining Native American lands by the tribes, and a political and military confederacy (union) of tribes under his leadership. Soon government officials became alarmed at the growing number of warriors arriving at Greenville. William Henry Harrison (1773–1841), governor of the Indiana Territory, closely watched the Greenville community from his headquarters at Vincennes. He often sent messages to the tribes, inquiring about their motives. Tecumseh and Tenskwatawa assured the governor that they had peaceful intentions.

Move to Tippecanoe

By 1808 game and other resources at Greenville had been depleted, and the tribes were having difficulty supporting a growing population. Tecumseh and his brother moved the community to a site on the Tippecanoe River where the Tippecanoe meets the Wabash River. The men called the new village "Tippecanoe" or "Prophetstown." The location was ideal because fish and game were plentiful and the Indians were farther away from the white settlers. They were still under the wary eye of Harrison, however, who carefully monitored their movements.

Tecumseh continued to seek support for his confederacy. In the fall of 1808 he traveled to Canada and established political links with the British. During the next three years, he traveled widely among the tribes in the northwest and the south in search of recruits. He had only mixed success. Older leaders, particularly the "government chiefs" (the Indian name for native leaders who had dealings with the Americans), felt threatened by Tecumseh's leadership and warned their followers against him. Many chiefs did not want to unite with ancient enemies in other tribes.

Meets with Harrison

Tecumseh gained more followers with the unwitting help of Governor Harrison. In September 1809 Harrison entered into new land negotiations with the government chiefs. The result was the Treaty of Fort Wayne, which gave the United States two and a half million acres of Native American land. As word of this agreement spread among the northwestern tribes, warriors became disgusted with their leaders and joined Tecumseh's cause.

The following year Harrison made a final effort to subdue the native peoples without warfare. He suggested that Tenskwatawa visit Washington to meet the president. Instead, Tecumseh and several hundred warriors went to Vincennes to deliver a reply to Harrison. At Vincennes, Tecumseh and Harrison met for the first time. The men held a council in which Tecumseh spoke at length, reciting the long list of injustices that had been committed against the native people. He emphasized his opposition to the Treaty of Fort Wayne and admitted that he headed a confederacy dedicated to preventing further invasion of Indian lands. He concluded by saying that he was not at that time able to accept the invitation to Washington. Harrison came away from the meeting convinced that it was Tecumseh, not his brother, who was the real power in the Tippecanoe community.

The Battle of Tippecanoe

By 1811 Harrison had become openly hostile toward the Indians at Tippecanoe. Tecumseh was absent from the village at the time because he was recruiting among the tribes of the south. On September 26, Harrison took advantage of this opportunity by marching his army toward Tippecanoe. As Tenskwatawa watched Harrison's progress, he prepared for war. He took no action, however, until November 6, when Harrison's forces crossed the river and camped within a mile of the village. During the night the warriors surrounded the army camp, then made an attack before dawn. The Battle of Tippecanoe lasted just over two hours. Tenskwatawa's men then began to disengage, even though they had inflicted heavy losses on Harrison's troops. As the Indians abandoned their village, Harrison's men burned Tippecanoe. Although the Battle of Tippecanoe was not the glorious victory for the Long Knives that Harrison later claimed, the defeat was a severe blow to the absent Tecumseh. The event ended the career of Tenskwatawa, who had taken no active role in the fighting.

Supports British in War of 1812

Following the battle, Tecumseh established a temporary village on nearby Wildcat Creek and set about rebuilding his confederacy. His plan included appeasing the Americans. He assured Harrison that he would give careful consideration to a renewed invitation to visit Washington. As the possibility of war between Britain and the United States grew nearer, both sides courted the support of the northwest tribes. (The War of 1812 was an armed conflict that took place between the United States and Great Britain from 1812 to 1815. The main issue of the war was control of certain territories.) For Tecumseh the choice was not difficult. In June 1812, he headed for Canada,

THE SHAWNEE From prehistoric times the Shawnee had inhabited the Ohio valley. White frontiersmen (called "Long Knives" by the Shawnee) began settling the region in the eighteenth century. In the beginning, the Shawnee had good relations with the settlers. By the 1760s and 1770s, however, white settlers began arriving in ever-increasing numbers. They established permanent settlements, clearing and fencing the land and driving away the game (wild animals hunted and killed for food) on which the Shawnee depended. The Shawnee objected to this intrusion, and in 1774 a war broke out between the tribe and the Long Knives. When the colonies went to war with Great Britain in 1776, the Shawnee remained neutral (they did not take sides). The following year, however, their principal chief, Cornstalk, was murdered by white settlers during a peace mission. The Shawnee retaliated by killing many settlers.

In 1779, the Long Knives responded with an attack on Chillicothe, the principal Shawnee village, in present-day Ohio. Although the Shawnee easily repulsed the attack, the incident resulted in the splitting of the tribe. Nearly 1,000 Shawnee migrated to southeastern Missouri. After the American Revolution (1775–83) the new government acquired more Native American land to satisfy settlers and to recover financial losses from the war.

where he offered his support to the British. As American troops under General William Hull (1753–1825) advanced toward Detroit in present-day Michigan to protect American interests (see "Military" entry), Tecumseh sought support for the British cause among the various tribes.

Many of the tribes in the region made no distinction between the British and the Americans. Yet Tecumseh, by the force of his personality, won many converts. He led warriors in a number of successful engagements in Canada and the Detroit area. At the Battle of Brownstown, he turned back an army of over 150 American troops with only 24 warriors. Shortly afterward he was slightly wounded at the Battle of Monguagon.

Tecumseh was pleased when General Isaac Brock (1769–1812) took command of the British base of operations at Fort Malden in Canada. Brock's forceful manner won Tecumseh's immediate approval. The general had similar confidence in Tecumseh, who was given the rank of brigadier general. Brock informed the Shawnee leader of his plans to march on Detroit and placed him in command of all the tribal forces. Tecumseh played a pivotal role in the British conquest of Detroit on August 15.

Brock was killed in October and was succeeded by Colonel Henry Procter. Although Tecumseh had less confidence in Procter's abilities, he and his men remained with the British forces. After the British naval defeat at the Battle of Lake Erie, Procter announced his intention to abandon Fort Malden. But Tecumseh made such an inspiring speech before the assembled British and Indian troops that Procter reconsidered his position. He agreed to withdraw to Chatham instead and make a stand against the approaching American forces led by Harrison.

Tecumseh killed

Proctor retreated to Moraviantown as Tecumseh's forces guarded the rear. The colonel finally made a stand at the Thames River. The British quickly collapsed under pressure, however, thereby allowing American troops to surround the warriors' positions. During the battle, Tecumseh was fatally wounded by a bullet in the chest. The Indians gradually withdrew, and the Battle of the Thames ended in an American victory.

Although the Indian movement ended with the death of Tecumseh, he remains one of the most memorable figures in American history. Harrison once described the war chief as "one of those uncommon geniuses, which spring up occasionally to produce revolutions and overturn the established order of things." Tecumseh never wrote down his own words because the Shawnee did not have a written language. His story survived, however, through the voices of his white opponents, who respected him as a great warrior and worthy adversary.

FOR FURTHER REFERENCE

Books

Cwiklik, Robert. *Tecumseh: Shawnee Rebel.* New York City: Chelsea House, 1993.

Eckert, Allan, W. *A Sorrow in Our Heart.* New York City: Bantam, 1992.

The Fall of Detroit

AUGUST 16, 1812

The fall of Detroit was one of the crucial American military failures in the War of 1812.

The fall of Detroit took place early in the War of 1812, after the British defeated the defending forces of American General William Hull. Detroit was strategically located on the Canadian border, making it an excellent place for Hull to retreat to when his plan to raid British-held Fort Malden was a failure. Several factors contributed to Hull's unsuccessful Canadian campaign, including a disobedient militia contingent from Ohio and the *Cayacauga* incident (in which British forces captured an American ship). Ultimately, however, it was Hull's cowardice that caused him to flee to Detroit and then suddenly surrender the town after the British fired only one shot.

Preparations for attack on Canada

The War of 1812 was an armed conflict that took place between the United States and Great Britain from 1812 to 1815. A major catalyst for the war was America's wish to take over territory in what is now the western United States. Before the war, American frontiersmen traveled openly through land that was claimed by the British government. Over time, however, the British and their Native American allies began to confront the frontiersmen, treating them as trespassers. This led America to declare war on Britain on June 18, 1812. As part of

Appointed by President Thomas Jefferson, General William Hull was in charge of the American force selected to lead an assault on Fort Malden in Canada.

their military offensive, the American forces planned a major attack on Canada from three separate points on the border: the American fort at Detroit in Michigan Territory, the Nevada Territory, and Lake Champlain in present-day upstate New York.

Since the Americans outnumbered the British, the chances for a successful attack on Canada looked very good. In 1812 the American army numbered 185,000 men, including regulars (dependable soldiers), militiamen (inexperienced fighters), and short-term volunteers. The British, on the other hand, had only 12,000 soldiers; as a result, they were forced to recruit Native Americans who were not accustomed to European methods of warfare.

The *Cayacauga* incident

In 1805 President Thomas Jefferson (1743–1826) selected Hull to lead an attack on Fort Malden in Canada. (Fort Malden was on the site of present-day Amherstburg in southeast Ontario.) Hull's mission, however, was doomed from the start. In order to attack Fort Malden, he had to march his troops approximately 300 hundred miles to Canada from a camp in Urbana, in central Ohio. Hull left Urbana on June 15, 1812, three days before war had even been declared. He brought with him 2,075 unreliable Ohio militiamen who barely managed to march three miles a day. While traveling, Hull and his men had to endure pouring rain, mosquitos, and Indians who spied on them, but never attacked.

On June 27, almost two weeks after he had set out from Urbana, Hull was finally near Lake Erie. (At this time Hull had still not been officially informed that the war had begun.) As he approached the lake, Hull spotted a large ship called the *Cayacauga* anchored in a river. Since the ship flew an American flag, Hull decided to requisition (hire) it for sixty dollars. Hull wanted the *Cayacauga* to carry his army's cargo, which included medical supplies, tools, and important documents relating to the military campaign. Because Hull did not know that the war had started, he had no idea of the risk he was taking, especially since the American cargo would be very valuable to the British.

On July 1, the *Cayacauga* was captured on the Detroit River by the British at Fort Malden. There were no casualties in the takeover, but now the British had important information about America's attack plans. The next day Hull was informed that the war between America and Britain had begun. He was also told by friendly Native Americans that the *Cayacauga* had been captured. On July 6, Hull sent some of his officers to Fort Malden to retrieve the cargo. The officers learned that everything had been sold off, and that the money had been distributed among the British soldiers. The *Cayacauga* incident was to have a direct impact on Hull's plan to attack Fort Malden.

Hull attacks Fort Sandwich

Now that Hull was so far north, he was in a perfect position to attack Fort Malden. Not surprisingly, however, the Ohio militia was unprepared to fight. As a result, on July 7, Hull decided not to assault the British fort and to proceed instead to the American fort at Detroit. Once Hull and his army reached Detroit, he felt much safer. Hull now had 2,000 soldiers and the strength of Detroit's fortifications to protect his militiamen. Despite this feeling of safety, Hull still faced important problems. The main concern was that, because Fort Malden was located south of Detroit, British forces would be able to interrupt American supply routes from Ohio. Detroit heavily depended on this supply line, and now that there were more mouths to feed, it became even more crucial. Since he was under orders from Washington to engage the enemy, Hull had to attack the British even though he knew it would be difficult.

General Hull had three solid plans of attack. The first involved developing the militia into regular soldiers who would be competent enough to attack Fort Malden. The problem with this idea was that it would give the British time to train their own militia as well. It would also give British forces an opportunity to overtake the precious Ohio supply route, thus forcing the American army at Detroit to surrender due to starvation. Hull's second plan was to attack Fort Sandwich, a British fort located just across the Detroit River. This was a dangerous strategy, but it looked feasible because the Americans outnumbered the British. Hull's third—and probably safest—

plan was to retreat for supplies to a station at Miami Rapids (on the Great Miami River) in northwestern Ohio.

Despite the wisdom of his third plan, Hull decided to go with the second strategy and attack the British at Fort Sandwich. A victory there would secure American dominance on both sides of the Detroit River. Unfortunately, there was no victory for the Americans at Fort Sandwich. In fact, there was not even a battle. On the morning of July 12, Hull rallied his troops and crossed the Detroit River to assault the fort. To his surprise, the fort was deserted. The British had abandoned Fort Sandwich and retreated south to Fort Malden. Suddenly, Hull found himself in a precarious position.

The British grow stronger

After the mix-up at Fort Sandwich, Hull could have turned south to attack Fort Malden, but he retreated once again to the safety of Detroit. By now his military strength was declining. Not only was the enemy a threat, but his own army was turning against him. The Ohio militia wanted Hull ousted from command—they even convinced the soldiers at Detroit to turn against the failing leader. In the meantime, the British were growing stronger. They were under new leadership and had managed to recruit more troops, including militiamen and Native Americans. The British commander, Isaac Brock (1769–1812), had just arrived at Fort Malden, bringing with him the great Shawnee chief Tecumseh (1768–1813) and his men. Brock had persuaded Tecumseh to help him capture Detroit.

Hull felt this increase in British strength when the enemy tightened its grip on the American supply line to Detroit. Finally, Brock decided to attack Detroit. He advanced to Fort Sandwich and waited with the newly replenished British army. At the same time, Hull was struggling to maintain control over both his men and his sanity. The Ohio militia continued to prove troublesome, and supplies from the south were regularly being intercepted. On August 14 Hull sent Colonel Lewis Cass (1782–1866) and another officer named McArthur out with a party of soldiers to escort a northbound supply train that was encountering enemy ambushes. Subsequent events would prove this to be a fatal error. Hull was now left to face Brock's psychological tactics of all by himself.

TECUMSEH Tecumseh (c. 1768–1813), the chief of the Shawnee tribe, was probably born in Clark County, Ohio. He gained fame among Native Americans as a mighty but humane warrior. (He did not, for example, condone the torturing of prisoners.) When the United States government began seizing Native American land, Tecumseh asserted that the land could not be turned over or even purchased because it belonged to all Native Americans. The United States did not accept this position, however, so Tecumseh organized tribes in the Northwest, the South, and the Mississippi Valley to protect Native American territorial rights. This alliance failed in 1811 when Tecumseh's brother, Tenskwatawa (c. 1768–1834; also called "Shawnee Prophet"), was defeated at the Battle of Tippecanoe (site of present-day Tipp City, Ohio).

This defeat brought about the downfall of the Native American military effort. Tecumseh then allied the Shawnee with the British in the War of 1812 and was named a brigadier general. He went on to lead several successful campaigns before being killed during an American defeat of British troops at the battle of the Thames in 1813. The subject of numerous books and dramas, Tecumseh is featured in *The Frontiersmen* (1967), a popular historical narrative by Allan W. Eckert.

Psychological warfare

In an attempt to undermine Hull, Brock dressed Fort Sandwich villagers in British military red coats to make it seem like the Americans were outnumbered. When Brock demanded a surrender and Hull refused, British warships on the river fired their mighty guns into the air. Probably the most difficult turn of events occurred when McArthur and Cass came back to Detroit, but camped three miles outside the town. For some reason—either spite or neglect—the men failed to inform Hull that they were nearby, thus leaving the declining general to fend for himself when he needed military support the most.

The British take Detroit

The British attacked Detroit on the morning of August 16, 1812. Around 3:00 A.M., Hull spotted British soldiers advancing in formation flanked by many Native Americans. The enemy force was strong, and the frightened commander had only a few options for retaliation. At that moment, Hull wanted to surrender Detroit to spare the townspeople. He decided against it, however, because in doing so he would be giving up without a fight. Hull therefore settled for a third plan, which

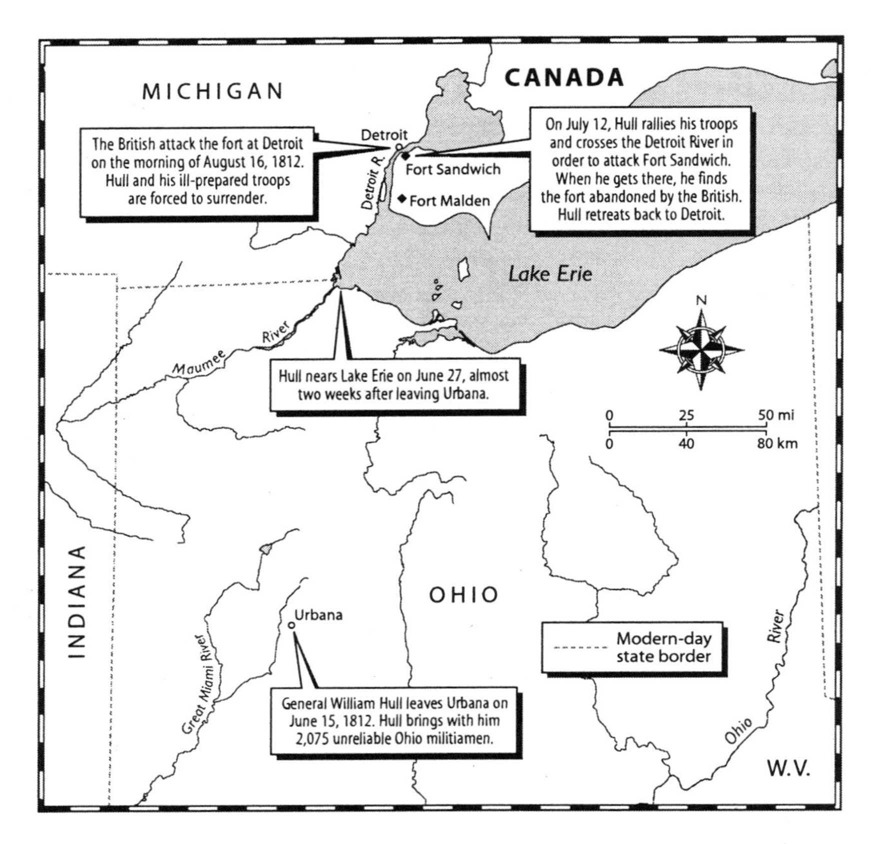

General William Hull's forces were eventually forced to retreat to Detroit and wait for reinforcements. The reinforcements never appeared and Hull gave up the fort to the British with little resistance.

was to huddle inside the fort and wait for McArthur and Cass to return with stronger soldiers.

Hull did not have to defend Detroit for long because the battle was over very quickly. As soon as the British fired a shell into the center of the fort and killed a few Americans, Hull surrendered. After the fall of Detroit, the American regular soldiers were captured by the British and became prisoners of war. For some reason, the Ohio militiamen were sent safely back home. Hull was taken prisoner by the British and shipped off to Canada. Later, after his release, Hull was court-martialed for cowardly conduct. Because Hull had fought so well in the American Revolution, however, President James Madison (1751–1836) dismissed the charges. Nevertheless, Hull's surrender at Detroit seriously damaged American morale early in the War of 1812.

GENERAL WILLIAM HULL

William Hull (1753–1825) was born in Derby, Connecticut. After graduating from Yale College, he practiced law. Hull later served his country as a soldier during the American Revolution (1775–83). In 1805 Hull was named governor of the Michigan Territory by President Thomas Jefferson. At age fifty-eight, Hull became a general in the War of 1812 and led the unsuccessful invasion of Canada that resulted in the fall of Detroit on August 16, 1812.

Historians cite several reasons why Hull's raid on Canada failed. One major factor was Hull's reliance on an unstable Ohio militia. Since militiamen were inexperienced recruits, they tended to be unreliable on the march and in battle. The Ohio militia members were particularly problematic for Hull. For example, the recruits could not understand why their general would not let them "tar and feather" one of their officers. (Tarring and feathering was a common form of punishment that involved dipping the wrongdoer in tar, then covering the tar with feathers.) Yet when the Ohio militia mutinied (rebelled), Hull did not punish the men. Ultimately, perhaps because of his age, Hull was too easygoing on the troublemakers from Ohio.

Was Hull a scapegoat?

Despite the fact that Hull made mistakes during his military expedition to Canada, he should not bear all the blame for the failure at Detroit. In fact, some historians consider Hull a scapegoat for certain problems inherent in the American military structure of the time. While Hull lacked certain leadership qualities, he was also given the impossible task of commanding a notoriously disobedient—and vastly undertrained—militia. The conduct of Hull's officers was also less than professional, as evidenced by the actions (or rather, inactions) of McArthur and Cass.

The fall of Detroit was only part of the widespread failure of the American military early in the War of 1812. Because its army lacked solid leadership and training, America was not militarily prepared to battle a more organized foe. In fact, by August 1814, the British had used their advantage to take Washington, D.C. Angry British troops then burned the White House and the Capitol building. American fortunes improved by the end of the year, however, and the United States signed a treaty with the British on December 24, 1814. The treaty brought an end to hostilities, returned disputed land to the United States, and ordered the formation of commissions to settle boundary disputes. General Andrew Jackson (1767–1845) led the final action of the War of 1812, when he defeated the British at the Battle of New Orleans in Louisiana two weeks later, on January 8, 1815.

FOR FURTHER REFERENCE

Books

Regan, Geoffrey. *Snafu: Great American Military Disasters.* New York City: Avon Books, 1993, pp. 83–95.

The Battle of Waterloo

JUNE 18, 1815

Napoléon's defeat gave rise to a figure of speech—"to meet one's Waterloo"—that is now commonly used to describe a crushing defeat.

The defeat of France by Allied forces at Waterloo, Belgium, in 1815 ended twenty-three years of warfare in Europe. The engagement is best remembered, however, as the fall of Napoléon Bonaparte. In 1800 the legendary Corsican-born general rose to power in France; by 1810 he had conquered most of Europe. Four years later, however, the emperor's regime (or government) was toppled and he was forced into exile. In 1815 Napoléon returned to France and regained his rule for a period called the "Hundred Days." Napoléon expected the battle at Waterloo to be a definitive French victory, one that would again establish the emperor's power in Europe. Because of a tactical blunder on Napoléon's part, however, the conflict turned into a total disaster for France. It was also marked the end of Napoléon's political career. The emperor's misadventure at Waterloo eventually gave rise to a figure of speech—"to meet one's Waterloo"—that is now commonly used to describe a crushing defeat.

Early life and career

Napoléon Bonaparte (original Italian spelling, Napoleone Buonaparte; 1769–1821) was born at Ajaccio on the island of Corsica (a landmass off the west coast of Italy). His parents, Carlo and Letitia Bonaparte, were of Italian descent and moved

French emperor Napoléon Bonaparte was one of the most hated political leaders in Europe.

to Corsica when the island was still under Italian rule. In 1769, when France occupied Italy, Corsica became a part of France. Two years later Carlo took an administrative position with the French government, which entitled him to send his sons, Napoléon and Joseph, to the College d'Autun in France in 1778.

Although Napoléon received his entire education in France, he always considered himself a foreigner in that country. After a brief stay at Autun, he attended several military schools; he also read philosophy, literature, and politics. At age sixteen, when his father died, Napoléon became head of his family. After graduating from a military academy in 1785 he went back to Corsica. Napoléon returned to France in 1793 to fight in the French army against revolutionary forces during the French Revolution (1789–99; a movement to overthrow the monarchy and replace it with a democratic form of government).

In 1795 Napoléon was put in command of the French army in Europe. Over the next few years he led several military expeditions, including an unsuccessful mission in Egypt and Syria where his forces were defeated by British troops. Shortly after this defeat, Napoléon participated in a coup (a military revolt) to overthrow the Directory (revolutionary) government. By 1804 he was emperor of France.

Napoléon conquers Europe

By the time Napoléon initiated the battle of Waterloo on June 18, 1815, he was one of the most hated political leaders in Europe. Small in stature but possessing a big ego, Napoléon was often called the "Little Corporal." After crowning himself emperor in 1804 he made numerous reforms in government and education. He also waged several successful battles, consolidating virtually all of Europe into the Napoleonic empire. Many vassal (dependent) states were headed by Napoléon's relatives, and treaties brought numerous other countries under his direct control.

In 1810 Napoléon discarded his first wife, Joséphine (born Marie Joséph Rose Tascher de la Pagerie; 1763–1814) because she could not give him a son who would become the heir of the empire. That same year Napoléon married Marie Louise (1791–1847), the daughter of Emperor Francis I of Austria (1768–1835), thus forming an alliance with Austria. In 1811 Marie Louise had a son, Napoléon II (1811-1832), whom Napoléon named king of Rome.

Suffers a decline

Napoléon's decline started with his defeat by Russia in 1812. After his defeat, the people of Europe began turning against the emperor. When he experienced several other military losses, the French also became disenchanted with Napoléon's rule. In 1814 Austria, Russia, Prussia, and Great Britain (called the Allies) persuaded the French to remove Napoléon from the throne and exile (send into forced absence) him to Elba (an island in the Mediterranean Sea off the west coast of Italy). Under the treaty of Fountainebleau, the Allies gave Napoléon Elba plus an annual income of two million francs and four hundred guards. He was also allowed to retain the title of emperor. The new French government (called the Bourbon Restoration) was not welcomed by French citizens, however, and soon Napoléon began plotting his return to power.

Hundred Days begin

On March 20, 1815, less than a year after retreating to Elba, Napoléon went back to Paris (the capital of France). He managed to reach France with the aid of several of his Elba guards. Along the way republican peasants rallied to his cause, and he even recruited the soldiers who came to arrest him. Within a short time Napoléon had established his own Restoration government. Thus began the Hundred Days, the name given to the three months of Napoléon's second reign. The emperor now promoted himself as a friend of the people, not as a dictator. Yet his regime differed little from that of the Bourbons, and again the citizens became disillusioned.

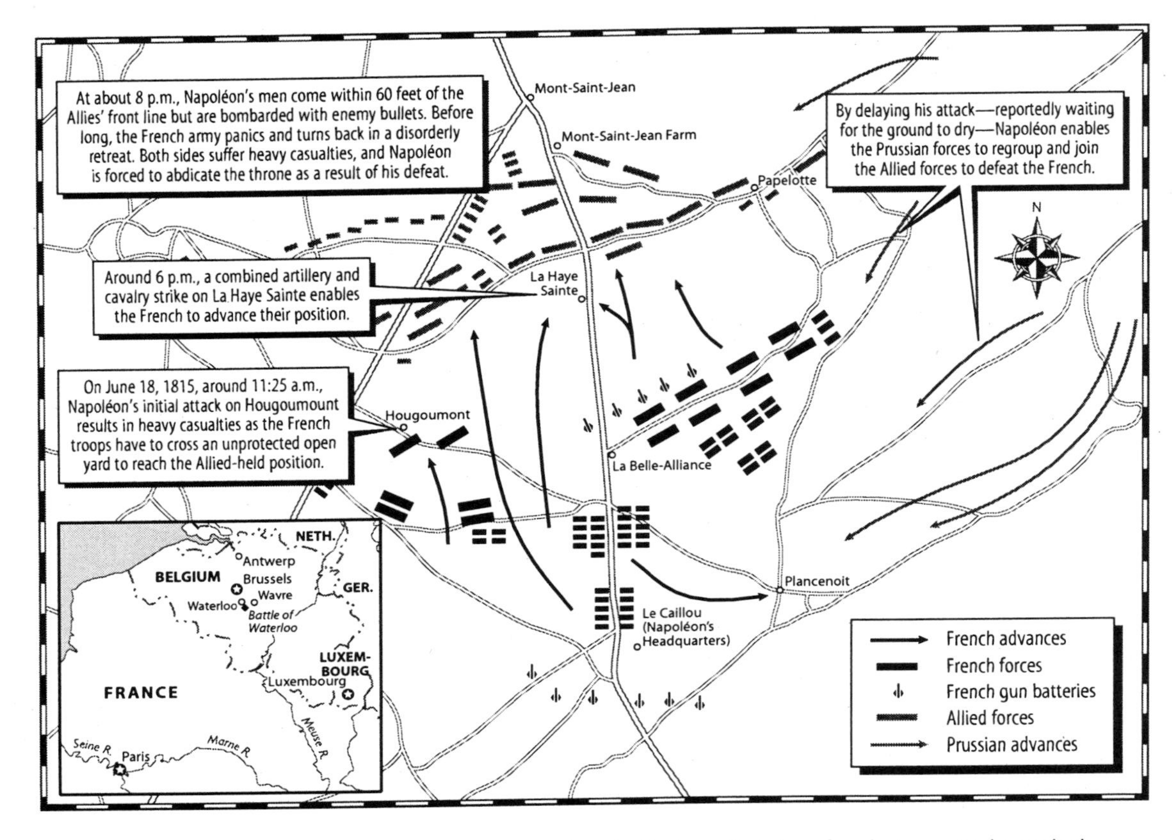

French troops under the leadership of Napoléon Bonaparte lost the Battle of Waterloo after their commander made the troops wait for the battlefield to dry out.

Another problem was that Allied and Prussian troops were gathering in countries around the borders of France. Napoléon quickly organized an army and marched into Belgium to head off the main Allied and Prussian forces. On June 16, 1815, Napoléon's generals Michel Ney (1769–1815) and Emmanuel de Grouchy (1766–1847) defeated Prussians under the command of Gebhard Leberecht von Blücher (1742–1819) at Ligny (a village south of Brussels).

Ney and Grouchy had successfully separated the Prussian army, but had failed to annihilate it completely. Napoléon therefore prepared to attack the Allies three miles south of the village of Waterloo (about eight miles northeast of Ligny) two days later. He was confident that his army could easily win against the combined Allied forces, which were commanded by British general Arthur Wellesley, first Duke of Wellington

(1769–1852). Napoléon fully expected to advance seventeen miles to the north after the defeat and quickly seize Brussels, the capital of Belgium.

Wellington gains advantage

Napoléon and Wellington were both legendary military heroes, but the two men had never met in battle. Napoléon made his first error in underestimating the abilities of the brilliant British general. In fact, Napoléon voiced disdain for Wellington's victories in India, which he regarded as an inferior arena for war. Napoléon also knew from the outset that his army was superior to the Allied forces. Wellington's soldiers were mostly young, inexperienced recruits who had never even witnessed gunfire in a hostile situation. Nevertheless, Napoléon inadvertently let Wellington gain a significant advantage: choosing the battle site.

Wellington massed his troops on a hill behind two farm complexes, La Haye Sainte at the center and Hougomount on the right. He then stationed soldiers in La Haye Sainte. He also placed 7,500 men in Hougoumont, a large stone structure surrounded by a wall that connected several buildings. Hougomont, which became the focus of the battle, was made into a fort under the command of Lieutenant Colonel James Macdonnell, a Scottish officer. Macdonnell's men broke double rows of loopholes (openings for guns) into the buildings and walls, from which they would fire to support the soldiers on the front line. Wellington's tactic would force the French to concentrate on taking the buildings, then to go uphill to reach the main line of Allied forces. An additional difficulty for Napoléon was that the battlefield itself was quite small, measuring only about six square miles.

Napoléon makes errors

Rain had fallen continuously throughout the day and night on June 17. By the next morning the battlefield was soggy. This was yet another factor that worked against Napoléon. No one now knows exactly when the Battle of Waterloo began on June 18, although most historians place the time at around 11:25 A.M. The crucial point, however, is that Napoléon reportedly waited to stage the attack on Hougomont until midday because

THE INFANTRY CHARGE Prior to the introduction of mechanized warfare in World War I (1914–18), the infantry charge was an important battle tactic used by military commanders. The infantry charge followed a period of bombardment by heavy artillery, such as cannons and large guns, which could fire long distances directly into enemy lines to reach concentrations of troops and equipment. After the bombardment, commanders would give the order to charge, and soldiers on foot (called infantrymen) would advance toward the enemy in wide, horizontal lines. The infantrymen were armed with rifles or hand guns that they fired when they were within striking range of the enemy's front line (which was also composed of advancing infantrymen). Once the men in the two lines met, they continued to fire their weapons or engage in hand-to-hand combat. Infantrymen also used bayonets, or knives attached to the end of a rifle barrel. Infantry charges were always bloody and resulted in extremely high casualties.

he wanted the ground to be dry. This delay gave Blücher time to regroup his Prussian army and move toward Waterloo to join Wellington's forces.

Napoléon made another mistake by not expecting the Prussians to take part in the battle. He assumed that Grouchy had removed them as a serious threat two days earlier, at Ligny. If any of Blücher's forces did remain, Napoléon reasoned, they would quickly be chased away by Grouchy and would not have any role at Waterloo.

The slamming of the gate

Napoléon was therefore confident of victory when he ordered his men to open fire on Hougomont. Backed by thunderous artillery (heavy weapons), thousands of French infantrymen (armed soldiers on foot) slowly moved toward the farm. At first Allied troops, forming a line of defense around Hougomont, drove the Frenchmen into a wooded area. But Napoléon's forces finally rallied and charged at the walls. When the Frenchmen came to a hedge (a row of bushes), they thought they were within easy reach of their target. They were very surprised to see they first had to cross an open, fifty-foot yard. This small area became a terrible killing field. Macdonnell's soldiers, firing their muskets (shoulder guns) from inside the buildings and walls, literally mowed down regiment after regiment of French troops.

The French managed to surround the farm, however, and around noon they stormed a gate into the Hougomont courtyard. A huge soldier nicknamed "l'Enfonceur" ("the Smasher") used an ax to break through the gate, and the French swarmed inside. They fought furiously in hand-to-hand combat with Allied troops. Almost immediately, however, Macdonnell (also a very large man) and several of his soldiers threw their weight against the gate, slammed it shut, and locked it with an iron bar. The fight in the courtyard continued until all of the French soldiers but one—a drummer boy—were dead. The slamming of the gate is considered a critical turning point in the Battle of Waterloo.

French suffer setbacks

In the meantime, Grouchy's 33,000-man army, which was nearly one-third of Napoléon's entire force of 105,000 men, had failed to chase off the Prussian troops. In fact, the French were trapped at Wavre, eight miles away, by 30,000 Prussians. Blücher's main force was on its way to join Wellington. The Prussians gradually arrived at Waterloo, putting severe pressure on Napoléon's army throughout the day. By 6:00 P.M. the French had staged four major attacks in an attempt to break through the Allied lines. But each of their efforts failed because there was no cooperation between the infantry and cavalry (soldiers on horseback). Eventually Napoléon was forced to move several battalions (units of soldiers) to prevent the enemy from penetrating his own lines.

Another Napoléon error

At 6:00 P.M. Napoléon ordered a combined infantry, cavalry, and artillery attack on La Haye Sainte. The French finally took the farmhouse, and nearly 10,000 Allied troops fled. A triumphant Napoléon pushed his army toward Hougomont, which was now on fire and nearly in ruins. As the French moved forward, they continued bombarding the center of Wellington's line. The Allies sustained extremely heavy losses and Wellington was running out of men. For the first time a French victory appeared to be at hand. At that point, however, Napoléon made a serious error. Ney, one of his two commanders, requested infantry reinforcements. But Napoléon was so preoccupied with fighting off a Prussian attack that he delayed sending Ney any extra men until after 7:00 P.M.. By then it was too late. All of the Prussians had arrived, giving Wellington a chance to regroup and strengthen his defenses.

Hundred Days end

Ney led the final French charge around 8:00 P.M.. When Napoléon's men came within sixty feet of Wellington's front line, the Allies opened fire. Hundreds of French infantrymen fell as they were pounded again and again by an unrelenting volley of bullets. Within fifteen minutes the Allied troops started moving forward while the Prussians attacked from the side. The French army panicked, turning back in a disorderly retreat as the Prussians followed in hot pursuit. After the last shot was fired, 25,000 of Napoléon's men were killed and wounded and 9,000 men were captured. Wellington's army also suffered heavy casualties—about 15,000 men—while Blücher's losses totaled 8,000 men.

On June 22, one hundred days after his return from Elba, Napoléon was forced to abdicate (give up) the throne for the second and final time. His son, Napoléon II, was named emperor. At first Napoléon intended to go to the United States. The British intervened, however, and sent him to Saint Helena (an island in the South Atlantic Ocean, west of Africa). Napoléon lived in splendid isolation until his death from stomach cancer in 1821.

FOR FURTHER REFERENCE

Periodicals

"Great Battles: The Age of Napoléon." *Cowles Enthusiast Media.* Summer, 1998.

The Crimean War

OCTOBER 1853 TO FEBRUARY 1856

During the Crimean War, an overwhelming number of soldiers died because of bureaucratic mismanagement.

Throughout history wars and specific battles have been notable for a variety of reasons. An engagement may have resulted in high casualties, for example, or a general triumphed because he employed a brilliant strategy. Few wars, however, are considered remarkable because they were terribly mismanaged, as was the case with the Crimean War (1853–56). While British forces won this two-year campaign against the Russians, they suffered numerous and highly preventable losses. The direct cause of these deaths was blatant neglect and mismanagement on the part of the British bureaucratic system, a structure that should have functioned in a more progressive and humane way.

The Crimean War

The Crimean War, which began in October 1853 and ended in February 1856, was fought on the Crimean Peninsula (a land area at the southern border of Russia in the Black Sea). The conflict involved Russia against Britain, France, and the Ottoman Empire in Turkey. Before the war, Nicholas I of Russia (1796–1855) began a dispute with France over Catholic churches that were located in Palestine (a region that is considered sacred by Christians, Jews, and Muslims). Britain entered the conflict because Russia wanted to control the Dar-

The Crimean War is widely considered one of the most mismanaged military campaigns of all time. Many soldiers lost their lives, not in battle, but as a result of starvation and disease.

danelles (a narrow strait of the Black Sea), which would have threatened British Mediterranean Sea routes. Austria also threatened to join the dispute because of Russia's growing influence in the Balkans (states on the Balkan Peninsula between the Adriatic and Balkan Seas). Even though Britain and France were very powerful enemies, it was Austria's presence that really frightened the Russians.

Britain's support gave Turkey the confidence to stand up to the Russians. In 1853, when the Russians had occupied the Danubian Principalities (present-day Moldavia and Walachia, on the Danube River in Europe), Britain persuaded Turkey to reject Russian demands. Then, on October 4, 1853, Turkey declared war on Russia. When the Russians destroyed a Turkish fleet on the Black Sea, Britain and France entered the war. They proceeded to wage a fairly successful campaign against

RUSSELL'S REPORTS It has been said that newspaper reporters love a good story. This seemed to have been especially true during the Crimean War. British military leaders were managing the campaign so poorly that the country's press ridiculed them daily. In 1854, William Howard Russell (1820–1907), a war correspondent (a reporter who sends stories from the battlefield) for *The Times*, became famous for his honest and realistic stories. Russell often used humor and satire to uncover British mismanagement in the field. One result of Russell's exposés, however, was the leaking of important military secrets and strategies. The Russians often got their hands on *The Times* before the British. On October 23, for instance, a British regiment was attacked by surprise. Military leaders were left wondering how the Russians knew so much about their location. Later, when the British troops discovered that their position had been given away by Russell in a news article, they were furious. Despite their complaints, however, government officials in London never censored Russell's reports. The enemy continued to receive information, leading one Russian to say, "We have no need of spies, we have *The Times*."

Russia for the next two years. In 1856 Russia was forced to back down when Austria threatened to enter the war. On March 30, 1856, Russia signed the Treaty of Paris and gave up control of Turkey, the Danube River, and the Black Sea.

A cruelly mismanaged war

Despite the fact that the British were victorious, the Crimean War has gained dubious recognition as one of the worst-managed wars in history. The failure in Crimea took place on a grand scale and affected almost every soldier on the battlefield. A disproportionate number of deaths on both sides resulted from neglect and mismanagement. It has been reported that 250,000 British and Russian soldiers died from diseases linked to starvation. While the Russians were guilty of mismanaging certain aspects of the campaign, the British government was particularly irresponsible in its treatment of British troops.

Study finds massive starvation

Widespread starvation was the major issue during the Crimean War. In March 1855, two British officers, Colonel Alexander Tulloch and Sir John McNeill, investigated the causes of deaths among British soldiers. After visiting battlefield hospitals, Tulloch and McNeill discovered that soldiers were

Nurse Florence Nightingale introduced new battlefield hospital protocols that saved many soldiers during the Crimean War.

not dying not only from war wounds, but also from diseases related to starvation. At the end of their study, the officers concluded that a staggering thirty-five percent of the army was dying because of poor provisions. They found that the British Commissariats (the units in charge of storing and distributing food and supplies) simply were not supplying adequate food and clothing for soldiers who were forced to fight in a cold and wet environment.

Food not reaching soldiers

Tulloch and McNeill's most disturbing finding was that the Commissariat units had access to fresh meat, vegetables, and bread. Unfortunately, unit officials claimed that the fresh food was too difficult to distribute. When the Commissariats did dispense food to British troops, the soldiers got salt meat and biscuits, but no fresh vegetables. Tulloch and McNeill computed the actual nutritional weight of the food the British soldiers ate and compared it to other normal diets. They discovered that the average nutritional weight of provisions for a British sailor was 28.5 ounces. The nutritional weight of the food served to a Hessian soldier (a professional German trooper traditionally hired by the British) was 32.96 ounces. Tulloch and McNeill noted that the nutritional weight of the food for a Scottish prison inmate at the time was 25.16 ounces. Shockingly, the nutritional weight of the British soldier's diet in the Crimea was a mere 23.52 ounces.

Stories are scandalous

There were several scandals concerning the issuance of provisions to British soldiers. Many stories implicate one man in particular, Commissary-General Filder, as being responsible for many of the problems. For example, on November 4, 1854, a ship arrived at Balaklava (where the British camp was located) carrying 150 tons of badly needed vegetables. Because the

NURSE NIGHTINGALE In a war where nothing seemed to go right, Florence Nightingale (1820–1910; often referred to as the "Lady with the Lamp") became a legendary figure of compassion and order. Nightingale made revolutionary changes that vastly improved battlefield hospitals. Before she began her hospital service during the Crimean War, the conditions at British military clinics were horrible. For instance, hospital staff members made no effort to clean up the human waste and other filth that accumulated in areas where patients were treated. In fact, hospitals were so dirty that soldiers who came in with minor injuries often contracted infections. As a result, there was a disproportionate number of amputations due to gangrene (tissue decay). When Nightingale introduced standards for sanitation and efficiency, infection and death rates were dramatically reduced. Nightingale also organized a unit of thirty-eight nurses just to care for the severely wounded and dying. Before Nightingale arrived, all surgical operations were performed out in the open, in full view of frightened soldiers. Although she put up screens to hide these scenes, Nightingale unfortunately could not block out the screams.

ship did not have the proper paperwork, however, the vegetables were left to rot, never reaching the soldiers. On December 10, 1854, another ship with 278 cases of lime juice—a well-known cure for scurvy, a disease caused by lack of vitamin C—arrived at Balaklava. This shipment never left the boat because Filder failed to tell anyone it had arrived. Another outrageous story involved green coffee. Because Filder had requested that coffee beans be delivered unroasted, soldiers had to make coffee out of raw beans.

Shortage of greatcoats and boots

The climate of the Crimean Peninsula was cold and wet. As a result, winters there were very frigid. The British troops could have endured the Crimean winter, however, if they had been properly equipped. For a variety of reasons, the soldiers never received important essentials such as greatcoats (heavy overcoats) and boots. At the beginning of the war, when the soldiers arrived at Sevastopol (where the Russian camp was located), British commanders were so eager to attack that soldiers were ordered to leave their knapsacks behind on the transport ship. When the knapsacks were lost, important items such as uniforms and greatcoats were lost with them, never to be retrieved. In November 1854, a ship carrying 40,000 great-

THE CHARGE OF THE LIGHT BRIGADE One of the most infamous events in the Crimean War was the charge of the Light Brigade. On October 25, 1854, British general James Thomas Brudenell, Earl of Cardigan (1797–1868), led the Light Brigade, a unit of 670 cavalry troops (soldiers on horses), against the Russians at Balaklava (a section of the city of Sevastopol on the Crimean peninsula). Brudenell was notoriously arrogant and quarrelsome with his officers and men. On the day of the tragic assault, Brudenell's troops misunderstood the general's orders and charged against a heavily fortified Russian position. More than two-thirds of the British soldiers were killed or wounded. British poet Alfred Tennyson later wrote the classic poem "The Charge of the Light Brigade" in memory of the fallen troops. Two films, one released in 1936 and the other in 1968, also commemorate the notorious military blunder.

coats and enough boots for all the troops sank on the way to the Crimea. British law itself seemed to doom the soldiers to suffering and death. According to military regulations, no soldier could receive more than one greatcoat every three years. As a result, when 12,000 greatcoats finally did arrive, almost 9,000 of the warm coats remained in storage.

The fact that British soldiers went without good boots did not help matters. The cold and damp weather of the Crimean Peninsula caused the men's feet to swell, so that most of the boots did not fit. As a result, soldiers had to fight in boots that were much too tight. Because British officials were trying to economize, the boots were poorly made. The soles often fell off, or were pulled off by the deep mud that the troops had to march through. Not surprisingly, this hardship had a detrimental effect on British soldiers. After witnessing their Turkish allies grave robbing and stealing from corpses, British troops began to change their own behavior: they began to steal as well.

Might versus right

The Crimean War proved that modern battles are not necessarily more civilized, better organized, or less barbaric than their ancient counterparts. Although British forces won a hard-fought victory, the troops' negative Crimean experience raised questions about the price of that achievement. In the Crimea, administrative issues became as important as military strategy. The war proved that military campaigns had become very complex events, as dependent on a successful infrastructure (the support areas behind the scenes) as on well-trained fighting men.

FOR FURTHER REFERENCE

Books

Regan, Geoffrey. *The Book of Military Blunders*. Santa Barbara, CA: ABC-CLIO, 1991.

Francisco Solano López Destroys Paraguay

1862 TO 1870

Paraguay was almost destroyed when dictator Francisco Solano López went to war with Brazil, Argentina, and Uruguay.

Francisco Solano López was the extremely brutal dictator (absolute ruler) of Paraguay (a country in south-central South America) who nearly destroyed his own country during the Paraguayan War (1862–70). Fighting during the Paraguayan War led to a long series of setbacks for the poor nation, which was dominated by its stronger neighbors, Brazil, Argentina, and Uruguay. Each of the Paraguayan defeats tells the story of what happens when an unstable leader with poor military skills tries to achieve greatness.

The "Napoléon of South America"

López was neither a good president nor a skilled military leader. Physically unsuited for the role of a battlefield commander, he was grossly overweight and slow-moving. His greatest problem, however, was that he could not accept the fact that Paraguay was a small country and therefore no match for its larger neighbors to the south. López wanted to be the "Napoléon of South America." (Napoléon I, 1769–1821, was the emperor of France. A sometimes brilliant strategist, Napoléon met his most crushing defeat at the Battle of Waterloo [see "Military" entry].) López's Irish mistress, Eliza Lynch, was responsible for many of his grand ambitions. Claiming to be the niece of an officer who served with Horatio Nelson

(1758–1805) in the famous 1805 British victory at Trafalgar in Spain, she urged López on to similar military achievements.

Under Lynch's influence, López insisted upon getting involved in a civil war in Uruguay that also involved Brazil and Argentina. He wanted to become known as a great negotiator (a person who arranges compromises between parties), but instead doomed Paraguay to taking part in the war. López began fighting with Brazil in 1864, when he tried to place troops in the province of Corrientes in Argentina. By violating Argentinean neutrality (a position of not taking sides in a war), López ended up instigating the Brazil-Argentina-Uruguay alliance against Paraguay on May 1, 1865. Thus began the Paraguayan War (also called the "War of the Triple Alliance").

Francisco Solano López was the brutal dictator of Paraguay. During his regime, thousands of Paraguayan men lost their lives in the "War of the Triple Alliance."

Paraguay suffers

The people of Paraguay suffered under the leadership of López, whose motto was "Victory or Death." For instance, he pushed his soldiers so hard that many of them died needlessly. In battle, no Paraguayan was ever allowed to surrender. An example of López's overconfidence and brutality occurred when one of his officers, General Estigarriba, lost a battle at the beginning of the Paraguayan War. Back in Asunción, López and Lynch were preparing a grand celebration for Estigarriba. López was certain that the general was going to defeat the Allied troops (the combined forces of Brazil, Argentina, and Uruguay). When he received word that Estigarriba had retreated, however, López was furious. Fearing retribution (punishment), Estigarriba wisely decided not to return to Asunción. When López could not get his hands on the failed general, he executed the man's family instead.

Fights war himself

After the defeat of Estigarriba, López decided that if no one else could win against the Allies, he would fight the Paraguayan

FRANCISCO SOLANO LÓPEZ Francisco Solano López (1827–1870) was born in Asunción, Paraguay, the son of dictator Carlos Antonio López. When Carlos died in 1862, Francisco immediately set up a military dictatorship and proceeded to rule Paraguay for the next eight years. Unfortunately for the Paraguayans, their president was a man with delusions of greatness. López wanted to become the "Napoléon of South America," but he only brought shame and destruction to his country when he started the Paraguayan War (1862–70). During this conflict, which was also known as the "War of the Triple Alliance," Paraguay was nearly destroyed by Brazil, Argentina, and Uruguay. López was killed in 1870 at the end of the war.

War himself. Leaving Lynch in Asunción as his regent (a person who reigns in a ruler's absence), López set out for the battlefield. He was such a poor leader, however, that Paraguay suffered a major defeat as soon as he took over. In his first battle, at Tuyuty in 1866, López showed his heartlessness by marching his men straight into death. His forces were no match for the Brazilian artillery (a branch of an army that operates cannons or other large guns) who were firing grapeshot (a very deadly type of ammunition). Because López insisted on never surrendering, Paraguay lost 10,000 to 12,000 men.

Feeds enemy soldiers to crocodiles

Although López did not lose all of the battles in the Paraguayan War, his defeats outweighed his victories. When he won the Battle of Curupaity, for example, he lost only fifty of his own men and killed nine thousand enemy soldiers from Brazil and Argentina. Even this victory, however, was tainted by López's bloodthirsty actions. After the battle he threw all of the dead and wounded enemy soldiers to the crocodiles.

The more López lost, the more paranoid (excessively suspicious) he became. For instance, when López was nearly wounded by a shell from a Brazilian ironclad (a heavily armored boat), he thought the shell was specifically meant for him. In order to get revenge, he commanded his navy to destroy the entire Brazilian fleet. Unfortunately, the Paraguayan navy consisted of a few rafts that were no match for the huge ironclads, and the Paraguayan forces were defeated again. Since he was losing so badly, López feared that his men would attempt to overthrow him. Therefore, he selected certain soldiers as spies who were ordered to shoot anyone suspected of mutiny (rebellion). As a result, the Paraguayans were just as afraid of one another as they were of the enemy.

More atrocities against his own people

The war became an uninterrupted series of Paraguayan defeats until it reached a tragic end in 1870. A particularly crushing blow resulted from the siege of the Paraguayan fort at Humaita. The Paraguayan commander, Colonel Martinez, had been heroically defending the fort with only 400 men against 30,000 Allied troops. As was typical of López, he sent no support and would not let Martinez retreat. By this time the Paraguayan soldiers at the fort were starving so badly that they had to eat their own horses. Finally, after surrendering, Martinez mistakenly returned to López with the bad news. López shot Martinez and all his men, then executed their families.

In the meantime, Paraguay had all but lost the war. López ordered everyone to evacuate Asunción and march into the jungle. At one point López even considered asking the Paraguayans to commit mass suicide so that the enemy could not take them prisoner. He settled, however, for secretly throwing the national treasure of Paraguay over a cliff to hide it. López then threw all of the witnesses to this act over the cliff to keep the treasure's location a secret.

At the height of his insanity, López declared himself a "Saint of the Christian Church." When twenty-three Paraguayan bishops would not approve this declaration, López had them shot. After López pronounced himself a saint, his first matter of business was to punish his seventy-year-old mother with a public flogging (whipping). He was angry because she claimed that he was a bastard (a child born out of wedlock) and thus had no right to succeed his father, the previous president of Paraguay. Unfortunately, while these events were taking place, the Brazilians had begun raiding the Paraguayan camp. Just as López was about to execute his mother, a Brazilian soldier ran a spear through his stomach. López was so obese that he was not able to run from his attacker. As he lay on the ground, he fired several random shots at the soldier before dying from his wound.

ELIZA LYNCH Eliza Lynch was the mistress of Paraguayan president and dictator Francisco Solano López. A native of Ireland, she claimed to be the niece of a naval officer who fought with British hero Horatio Nelson during the English victory at Trafalgar, Spain, in 1805. Lynch played an important role in making López one of the cruelest military leaders in history. She filled his head with ideas of military conquest and fed his obsession to become as great as the French leader Napoléon I. When López decided to take over command of his forces during the Paraguayan War, he left Lynch in the capital at Asunción as his regent. Lynch organized the women of Paraguay into "Amazon" regiments. (Amazons were a race of female warriors in Greek mythology.) Equipped with weapons and lances (steel-tipped spears), the women fought under Lynch's command in many battles during the war. After the Brazilian attack in which López was killed (1870), the Amazons turned on Lynch. She was rescued by a Brazilian officer.

Paraguayans pay the price

The citizens of Paraguay paid the price for López's disastrous leadership. During the war the population of Paraguay fell from 1,337,000 to 221,000 people, and only 28,000 of the remaining inhabitants were adult males. According to some historical accounts, López's actions reduced the male population of Paraguay by almost ninety percent. Over time, many Paraguayans began to forgive López's cruelties. Some people saw their dead leader as a noble nationalist (a person devoted to the social and political interests of his or her country) whose love for Paraguay led to extreme measures in the battlefield. López's remains were eventually located in the national Pantheon of Heroes.

FOR FURTHER REFERENCE

Books

Byers, Paula K., and Suzanne M. Bourgoin, eds. *Encyclopedia of World Biography.* 2nd. ed. Detroit: Gale, 1998, pp. 507–08.

Regan, Geoffrey. *The Book of Military Blunders.* Santa Barbara, CA: ABC-CLIO, 1991.

The Assault on Fort Wagner

JULY 1863

"A war undertaken and brazenly carried on for the perpetual enslavement of colored men, calls logically and loudly upon colored men to help suppress it."

—Frederick Douglass

The ill-fated Union assault on Fort Wagner, a Confederate stronghold near Charleston, South Carolina, was a minor but highly significant battle in the American Civil War. Leading the Union charge on July 18, 1863, was the elite 54th Massachusetts Regiment (known as the "54th"), the first regiment of black soldiers from free states to serve in the line of battle. The commander of the 54th was Colonel Robert Gould Shaw, a white abolitionist (a person who was opposed to slavery). Abolitionists placed their hopes on the 54th, which had been formed to prove that black men could fight for the Union cause along with their white comrades.

When the 600 troops of the 54th stormed the fortress, the Confederates within opened heavy cannon and musket (rifle) fire. Within an hour, 272 men—including Shaw—had been killed. Although Union forces met defeat at Fort Wagner, the 54th had performed with great courage and bravery. The unit's heroic actions helped change public opinion about employing blacks in the military. (In fact, by the end of the Civil War 180,000 black men had served in the army and navy.) In this light, the failed assault on Fort Wagner could be considered a triumph. Yet, according to at least one soldier in the 54th, as well as historians who later studied the event, this political victory came at a tragic cost. Tactical errors placed the 54th in unnecessary danger, and lives were senselessly lost.

THE NEW YORK CITY DRAFT RIOTS The New York draft riots took place from July 13 to July 16, 1863, ending two days before the 54th Massachusetts Regiment's assault on Fort Wagner. The riots were sparked by the Union Conscription Act of March 3, 1863, which stated that all able-bodied men between the ages of twenty and forty-five could be drafted into military service. A drafted man could be excused, however, if he could find a substitute or pay the government $300. This legislation met with resistance throughout the North, but reactions were especially explosive in New York City, where many people sympathized with the South. Unskilled workers were enraged because they could not pay $300 to avoid service. When they were drafted the men could therefore lose their jobs to newly emancipated blacks.

On July 13 a mob of laborers overpowered the police and militia (state military forces) and seized the Second Avenue armory (a government building where arms and ammunition are stored). Targeting blacks and abolitionists in particular, the rioters beat people to death and burned a black orphanage. During the four days of chaos, businesses were destroyed and looting was rampant. Finally, on July 16, the army, navy, state militia, and West Point cadets restored order. More than 1,000 people were killed and property damage was estimated as high as $2 million. The New York City riots and the heroism of the 54th at Fort Wagner produced an outpouring of public sympathy for blacks in the North.

Emancipation an explosive issue

The Civil War (1861–65) was a conflict between the Northern states (also called the Union) and eleven states in the South that withdrew from the Union to form a separate government called the Confederate States of America (also known as the Confederacy). Although the war was fought over complex social and political issues, a primary focus of contention was the right of white southern plantation owners (people who ran large farms that grew mostly cotton) to use black slaves as workers. Abolitionists wanted the slaves to be emancipated (freed). Supporters of slavery contended that meddlers were not only trying to destroy the southern way of life, but were also intent on ruining the economic structure of the South.

Most abolitionists lived in the North, but this did not mean that all northerners sympathized with enslaved black people. In fact, there was intense racist sentiment among whites who considered blacks an inferior people. On January 1, 1863, U.S. President Abraham Lincoln (1809–1865) issued the Emancipation Proclamation, an executive order banning slavery in the Confederate States of America. By opening the way for blacks to move to the North and live as free men, the Proclamation unleashed extreme reactions among anti-emancipation factions. Unskilled white workers in industrial cities felt particularly threatened that blacks would take their jobs. Another sensitive issue was the Proclamation order that black men would serve in the U.S. armed forces. (Blacks had already been fighting in both northern and southern regiments, but this was the first law that enabled them to join regular military units.) Whites who opposed emancipation argued that blacks would never become competent soldiers and sailors, even with extensive training.

On January 1, 1863, President Abraham Lincoln issued the Emancipation Proclamation. This document was an executive order that freed slaves in Confederate territory.

First black regiment

The 54th Massachusetts Regiment was organized within weeks after Lincoln issued the Emancipation Proclamation. The abolitionist governor of Massachusetts, John A. Andrew (1818–1867), sent out a call for "persons of African descent [who would be] organized into separate corps." Andrew's goal was to prove that black men could be good soldiers. Aiding the recruitment effort was the Black Committee, which consisted of committed abolitionists. Among the committee members was George L. Stearns, the mayor of Medford, Massachusetts, who had assisted abolitionist John Brown in his attempt to end slavery (see "Society" entry).

The most prominent committee member was Frederick Douglass (1817–1895). A former slave who bought his own freedom, Douglass was the publisher of an abolitionist newspaper called *Frederick Douglass's Paper* in Rochester, New York. On March 2, 1863, Douglass printed an article titled "Men of Color, To Arms!" In the piece he appealed to black men to enlist. Douglass wrote: "The day dawns—the morning star is bright upon the horizon! The iron gate of our prison stands half open.... The chance is now given you to end in a day the bondage of centuries.... Remember Nathaniel Turner of South Hampton [see "Society" entry].... Win for ourselves the gratitude of our country—and the best blessings of our prosperity through all time." Two of Douglass's sons served in the 54th, and one was the regiment's first volunteer.

In an article printed on March 2, 1863, former slave Frederick Douglass urged black men to enlist in the 54th Massachusetts Regiment. One of Douglass's sons was the regiment's first volunteer.

Shaw heads the 54th

Another member of the Black Committee was Francis G. Shaw, a well-known white abolitionist. He persuaded his twenty-five-year-old son, Robert Gould Shaw, to accept the appointment as the commanding colonel of the 54th Massachusetts Regiment. (All of the twenty-nine other officers were also white.) Historians have noted that these men were showing unusual courage in leading the regiment because a large percentage of the public did not approve of blacks serving in the military. The general opinion was that blacks would not make good soldiers—a view that was to change dramatically after the assault on Fort Wagner.

54th wildly cheered

Following a period of rigorous training, on May 28, 1863, the 54th was formally presented to the governor. Crowds of spectators greeted the proud troops as they paraded in dark-blue dress uniforms through the streets of Boston. It was reportedly one of the most impressive events in the war. Shaw and his men then embarked by boat for Port Royal, one of several islands off the coast of the southern tip of South Carolina. The recruits were to support the Union campaign to capture Fort Wagner, a Confederate stronghold on Morris Island in Charleston harbor, and then take nearby Fort Sumter (a Federal fort seized by the Confederates at the beginning of the war). The ultimate goal was to occupy Charleston, a major Confederate supply port on the Atlantic Ocean.

ROBERT GOULD SHAW

Robert Gould Shaw (1837–1863) was born in Boston, Massachusetts, the son of Francis George Shaw and Sarah Blake (Sturgis) Shaw. His father was a prominent philanthropist (a person who supports charitable causes) and abolitionist. Robert entered Harvard College in 1856, then left in his third year to pursue a business career. A staunch patriot and abolitionist, Shaw enlisted in the Union Army at the outbreak of the Civil War in 1861. After being promoted to the rank of captain in the 2nd Massachusetts Infantry, he was wounded in battle at Winchester, Virginia. In February 1863 he accepted the assignment as colonel of the 54th Massachusetts Regiment, which consisted of black volunteers. Shaw was killed during the assault on Fort Wagner on July 18, 1863. He left behind his wife, Anna Kneeland (Haggerty) Shaw, whom he had married less than two months earlier.

First battle successful

When Shaw and his troops arrived at Port Royal, they had not been assigned to combat duty. Sixty miles to the north, on July 12, Union regiments staged an assault on Fort Wagner, but they were pushed back by Confederate gunfire. Union officers regrouped their forces and were working on another strategy. Then, on July 16, the 54th was attacked by Confederate troops on James Island, near Port Royal. Although the regiment was forced to retreat from battle, it inflicted heavy losses on the Confederates and saved three companies (units of soldiers) of the Union's 10th Connecticut Regiment. Impressed with the performance of his men, Gould received permission for them to join white troops under the command of General George C. Strong at Fort Wagner. For two days the 54th marched north along the Atlantic coast through mud and swamps. Hungry, exhausted, and soaking wet, they finally joined the other Union forces on the morning of July 18.

54th leads charge

Now part of Strong's main army, the 54th was designated to lead a second charge on the fort. According to the new plan, the men would head a column of around 4,000 (some accounts report 3,000) troops in regiments from Connecticut, New York, Pennsylvania, and Maine. The 54th would be the only black soldiers in the line of battle. Throughout the afternoon U.S. Navy gunboats and heavy-artillery units in Charleston

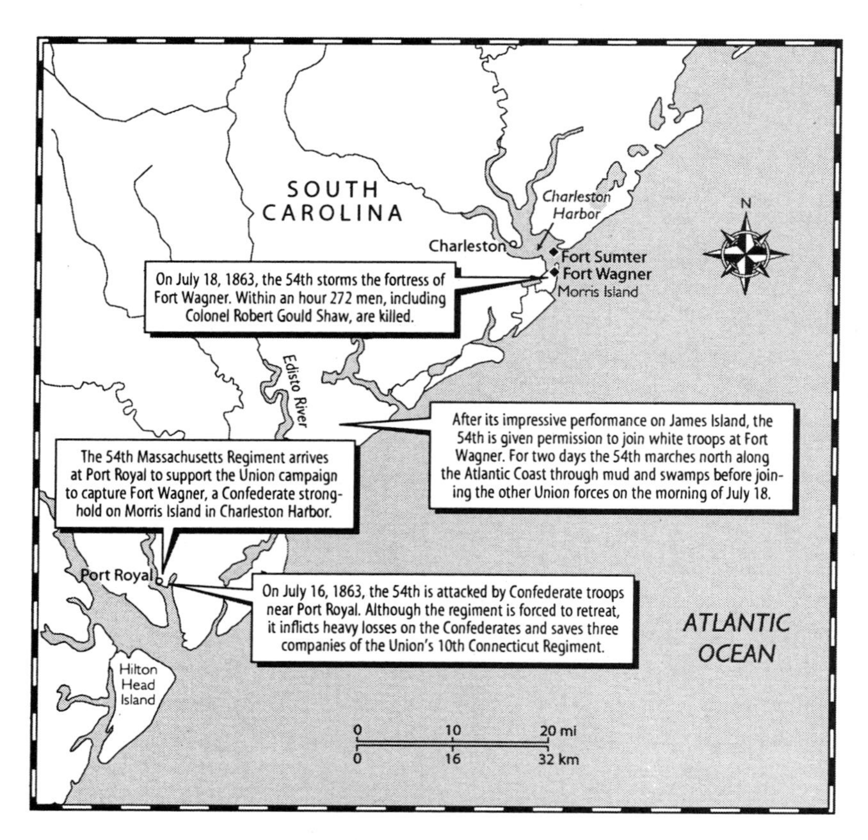

The 54th Massachusetts Regiment suffered severe casualties during an assault on Fort Wagner.

harbor pounded the fort with cannon shot. Around 8:00 P.M. in the evening, the 54th was given orders to begin the assault.

The soldiers of the 54th started marching toward Fort Wagner. When they were about 1,600 yards away, they made a battle formation of two lines, with Shaw heading the right wing (end) in the front. Urging his troops forward, he shouted, "We shall take the fort or die there!" As the troops advanced another 400 yards Confederate gunfire was surprisingly light. When Shaw gave the order to charge, the regiment moved in quick time (a rate of marching in which one hundred and twenty steps, each thirty inches in length, are taken in one minute). The soldiers then sped up their advance to double-quick time. As the 54th came within 100 or 200 yards of the fort, Confederate troops opened a thundering barrage of grapeshot (an especially lethal form of cannon shot) and musket fire.

Heroic in defeat

Amid wounded and dying comrades, troops of the 54th continued across a three-foot ditch of water and stormed the fort. Although they were repeatedly driven back and men were falling all around, the survivors ultimately surged over the wall. When the standard bearer (the soldier carrying the American flag) was hit by a bullet, the flag was instantly taken up by Sergeant William H. Carney. He himself had just been wounded, but he succeeded in planting the American flag on the wall. (Later, as Carney lay in a military hospital, he reportedly said, "Boys, the old flag never touched the ground.")

Victory amid heavy casualties

Shaw was now atop the wall. Just as he raised his sword and cried, "Onward boys!," he was fatally struck down. When the Union forces withdrew in defeat shortly thereafter, Shaw's body was left to be buried in a common grave. Later, after a truce was declared, Union officials offered to recover Shaw's body so his family could arrange a more appropriate burial. Francis G. Shaw responded, however, that his son had found a proper resting place, with his men.

Of the 600 men who led the charge on Fort Wagner, only slightly more than 300 survived. The 54th sustained the highest number of casualties as Union forces went down to defeat and the Confederates continued to hold the fort. Yet the battle was a political victory for Lincoln and supporters of emancipation. Not only had the soldiers fought competently and well, they had staged one of the most heroic battles of the war. Anti-black sentiment in the North was soon silenced. By the end of the Civil War, over 180,000 black soldiers and sailors had served in the Union cause.

A doomed attack

Some historians have questioned the tactical decisions that led to the ill-fated assault on Fort Wagner. Among the critics was Joseph T. Wilson, who served in Company C of the 54th Massachusetts Regiment during the siege. Wilson wrote *The Black Phalanx* (1890), an acclaimed history of black

Denzel Washington (center) and Morgan Freeman (far right) starred in *Glory,* a 1989 film about the exploits of the 54th Massachusetts Regiment.

soldiers who served in American wars (the Revolutionary War, the War of 1812, and the Civil War). In his book Wilson provided a vivid eyewitness account of the 54th's assault on Fort Wagner. According to Wilson, the U.S. Navy was responsible for the failure of the first attack, on July 12, 1863. Navy gunboats did not support the troops as they stormed the fort.

Wilson went on to state that lack of cooperation between the army and navy doomed the entire Union campaign at Charleston. "Had they been under the control of one mind," Wilson observed, "the sacrifice of life at the siege of Forts Wagner and Sumter [a later battle] would have been far less." Wilson also noted that the commanding general, George Gillmore, was receiving conflicting advice from his officers about when to attack. With great reluctance Gillmore finally gave approval for the charge to take place after dark. As a result, the Union troops had difficulty seeing their foe.

Final recognition

In 1884 the citizens of Boston commissioned American sculptor Augustus Saint-Gaudens (1848–1907) to create the *Shaw Memorial,* which now stands on Boston Common (a park in the center of the city). Edmonia Lewis (1845–c. 1909), an African-American sculptor, later made a bust (a replica of a person's head and upper shoulders) of Shaw that was placed in Memorial Hall in Cambridge, Massachusetts. In 1989, the 54th was memorialized in the film *Glory,* which told the story of the regiment's formation and bravery in battle. A memorial called *The Spirit of Freedom* was dedicated in 1998 in Washington, D.C. The statue commemorated all the African-American soldiers who fought in the Civil War.

FOR FURTHER REFERENCE

Books

Burchard, Peter. *"We'll Stand by the Union": Robert Gould Shaw and the Black 54th Massachusetts Regiment.* New York City: Facts on File, 1993.

Wilson, Joseph T. *The Black Phalanx.* New York City: Arno Press and *The New York Times,* 1890, reprinted and revised edition, 1968, pp. 249–64.

Pickett's Charge

JULY 1863

Following an order from General Robert E. Lee, General George Edward Pickett marched his Confederate regiment to certain death.

"Pickett's Charge" was a skirmish (one of a series of conflicts in a battle) at the Battle of Gettysburg during the American Civil War. During this fight 15,000 Confederate soldiers attacked a heavily defended Union position and lost. When the North retaliated, Union soldiers killed nearly half of the charging Confederates. Like many battle-related misadventures, Pickett's Charge was the result of overconfidence and lack of communication. The disaster ultimately stemmed from flawed Confederate military strategy and an ill-advised order from General Robert E. Lee.

The Civil War

The Civil War (1861–65) was a conflict in the United States between Northern states (also called the Union) and eleven Southern states that seceded (withdrew) from the Union and formed the Confederate States of America (also known as the Confederacy) with U.S. Senator Jefferson Davis (1808–1889) as president. Although the popular view is that the war was fought over slavery, the conflict was in fact the result of complex political, social, economic, and psychological differences between the North and the South. In 1860 the South was still an almost exclusively agricultural society based on plantations (large farms) worked by black slaves. The industrial and commercial North depended heavily on Southern cotton, but the North also had its own substantial agricultural economy.

Sectional differences between the North and the South had steadily grown since the American Revolution (1775–83; a movement by American colonists to gain independence from Britain). In particular, abolitionists (people who opposed slavery) argued that slavery should not be permitted in new Federal territories in the West. Hostilities increased after the Missouri Compromise of 1820, which admitted Missouri as a slave state and Maine as a non-slave state. When western non-slave states were admitted to the Union, many Southerners felt that their way of life was being threatened.

Major General George Edward Pickett led a deadly charge during the Battle of Gettysburg that left hundreds of Confederate soldiers dead.

Lee assembles his forces

In June 1863, two years after the beginning of the Civil War, the armies of the North and the South were almost evenly matched. The Union army commanded by General Ulysses S. Grant (1822–1885) was strong, but the Confederate forces led by General Robert E. Lee (1807–1870) had just won a series of small battles. As a result, morale was high among veteran soldiers in the South. The North, however, had a potential advantage because Grant had just seized Vicksburg (a Confederate fort located in Mississippi). If the Union army eventually succeeded in holding Vicksburg, the North would then gain control of the South.

Because Confederate morale was high, officers and soldiers were confident of their prospects for victory. President Davis had two choices. He could either order the army to stay and try to win back Vicksburg, or he could use his fierce commander Lee to launch a sustained attack on the North. Davis did not need to make a decision on his own because Lee stepped forward and offered a plan to invade Pennsylvania (the largest Union state, which bordered the Confederacy). The brash commander expected to strike such a powerful blow that Lin-

PICKETT SURVIVES GETTYSBURG Major General George Edward Pickett (1825–1875) was born in Richmond, Virginia. Pickett graduated last in his class from the United States Military Academy at West Point, New York, in 1846. Despite this dubious honor—which he shared with George Armstrong Custer—Pickett served with distinction in the Mexican War (1846–47). When the Civil War started, Pickett joined the Confederate Army. He was made a brigadier general in February 1862, and nine months later became a major general. Unfortunately, Pickett's major achievement was the crushing defeat that resulted from his marching a division of 4,300 soldiers into certain death during the Battle of Gettysburg. Surviving this debacle, Pickett continued to command troops until the end of war. Pickett then went on to work in an insurance business in Norfolk, Virginia, where he lived until his death.

coln would be forced to surrender. Dazzled by the plan, Davis agreed to it immediately and forgot about defending Vicksburg.

The army that Lee assembled for his invasion of Pennsylvania numbered 76,224 soldiers. He had several good commanders on his staff. James Ewell Brown "Jeb" Stuart (1833–1864) was the popular, colorful leader in charge of the 12,000-man cavalry (soldiers on horseback). Respected General James Longstreet (1821–1904) commanded the division headed by General George Edward Pickett (1825–1875), who had served with distinction in the Mexican War (1846–47). Longstreet disagreed with Lee's plan to invade the North, a scheme the general considered foolhardy. Longstreet was overruled, however, and Lee's plan was approved. Lee apparently failed to consider that his military council was much weaker without famous general Thomas "Stonewall" Jackson (1824–1863). Jackson had been killed in battle earlier that year at Chancellorsville, Virginia—Lee's first attempt to invade the North—and the Confederate army was suffering without him.

Lee has discipline problems

Almost as soon as Lee mobilized forces for the march into Pennsylvania on June 3, 1863, he began making mistakes. He had two major problems commanding his army. First, he was no good at giving orders. For instance, what Lee intended to be an order would often be taken as merely a suggestion by his junior officers. The other problem was insubordination (lack of respect for authority) among his soldiers. As a result, it often did not matter if Lee issued a strict order because his troops would do whatever they wanted.

One example of insubordination occurred soon after the Confederate army began marching north. Along the way, Lee gave permission for Stuart and the entire cavalry to raid Harrisburg, Pennsylvania. Since Stuart was not directly under Lee's command, he felt free to wage his own war. Stuart raided not only Harrisburg but also Washington, D.C. Stuart was gone so long that when Lee prepared for battle outside the town of Gettysburg, he had difficulty fighting until the cavalry arrived.

Robert E. Lee, commander of the Pennsylvania invasion, had several respected soldiers on his staff. Unfortunately, Lee's inability to issue direct orders to subordinates undermined his leadership.

A shortage of shoes

The Battle of Gettysburg began because the Confederate troops needed shoes. As Lee's army was marching through Pennsylvania, someone heard that a large supply of shoes could be found in the small town of Gettysburg. Since Confederate troops never had adequate footwear, an officer under the command of General Richard Ewell (1817–1872) led his unit into town to check out the rumor and commandeer any shoes they could find. About three miles outside Gettysburg the troops unexpectedly encountered the Union cavalry. This confrontation set off a call for reinforcements on both sides. Soon every Union and Confederate division in the area was moving toward Gettysburg. Ewell's forces pushed the Union troops south through town until the North forces managed to rally and take up positions on Culp Hill and Cemetery Hill south of Gettysburg.

Confederates hold off Union forces

Lee arrived at Gettysburg in the afternoon of July 1. Despite Lee's lack of control over his troops and the fact that the Union army was larger, the Confederates were initially successful. Ewell was in charge of the troops that "Stonewall" Jack-

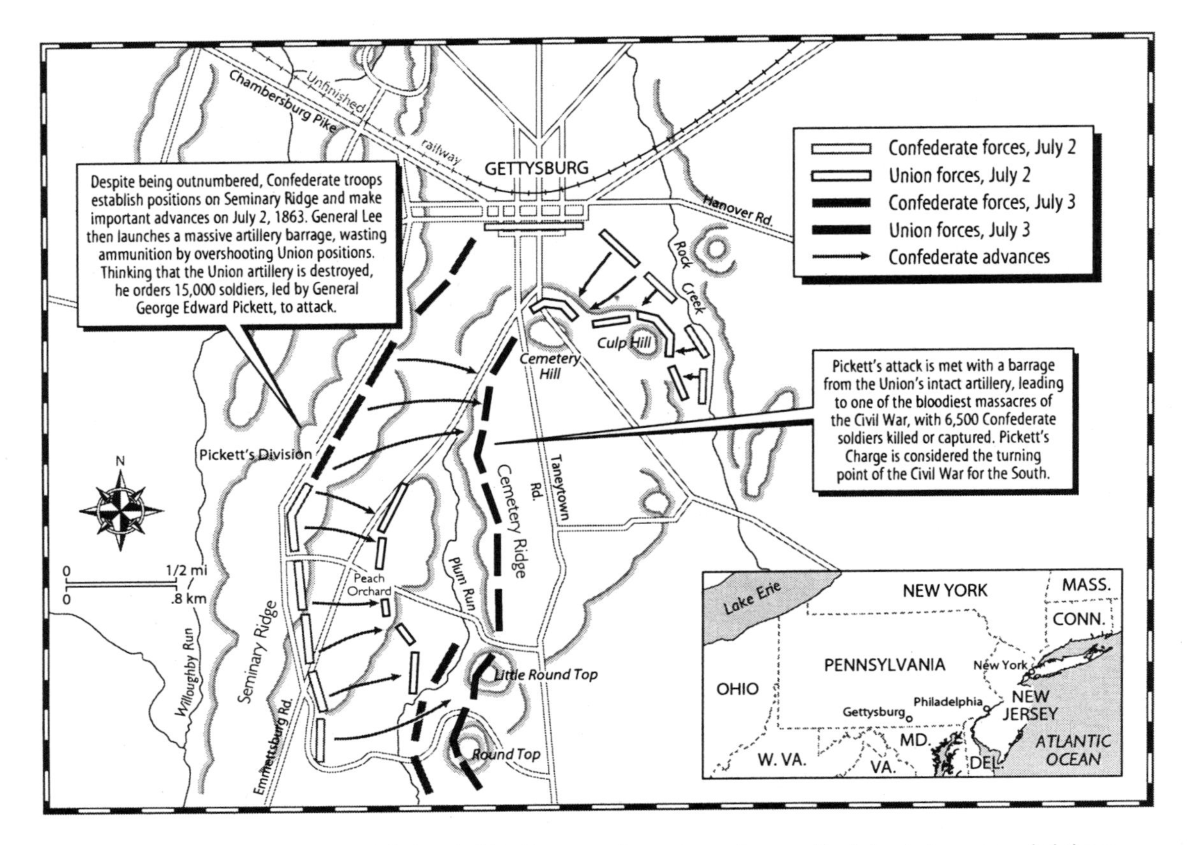

The Battle of Gettysburg, during which Pickett led his disastrous charge, began because Confederate troops needed shoes.

son commanded before he died. During the first day of fighting, Ewell managed to hold off Union forces on Culp Hill and was preparing for a full-fledged assault. Confederate fortunes changed, however, because of Lee's inability to give a direct order. Lee sent a message to the new commander "suggesting" that Ewell halt his advance and wait for reinforcements to arrive. Since Ewell was inexperienced—and because Lee had not given him a direct order— he did not know how to respond. As a result of Ewell's indecision, the Union ended up gaining a defensive advantage on Culp Hill.

Lee has conflict with officers

Another one of Lee's command problems was that when he gave a direct order, he expected the order to be carried out even if it was ill-advised. This is how Pickett's Charge

Gettysburg was the worst battle of the Civil War. The South suffered 28,000 casualties, while the North lost 23,000 men.

occurred. Lee wanted to seize Cemetery Ridge, a range of hills running directly south of the town. Even though Longstreet argued against the assault, Lee was obsessed with carrying out his plan. The Confederates had already performed well during the first day of fighting, and Stuart had finally returned with the cavalry. Lee hoped to turn these small advantages into an final victory.

By the morning of July 2, 65,000 Confederates were facing 85,000 Union troops. Despite the fact that the first day had gone fairly well for the Confederates, the second day ended in a stalemate. Confederate troops managed to take the Peach Orchard between Cemetery Ridge and Seminary Ridge, a range of hills directly to the west. Nevertheless, as a result of reluctance and indecision on the part of Longstreet and Ewell, the Union army gained an advantage not only on Culp Hill, but also on Cemetery Ridge. By the third day, July 3, the Confederate army was dug in on Seminary Ridge. Lee was exhausted but still insistent upon attacking Cemetery Ridge. This area was now occupied by strong Union forces under General George Meade (1815–1872), who had been in command for only five days.

Believing that the center of the Union line was weak, Lee planned a massive artillery (weapons) bombardment followed by a frontal (direct) attack by 15,000 soldiers led by Pickett's division of 4,300 men. Longstreet disagreed with Lee once again, arguing instead for an attack on the Union left flank (the end of the military formation). This exchange between Lee and Longstreet was the beginning of the end for the Confederate army. Unable to convince his senior officer not to attack the center, Longstreet departed and proceeded to go through the motions of carrying out Lee's unreasonable demands.

"General, shall I advance?"

On July 3, 1863, at 1:00 A.M., 138 Confederate cannons opened fire on the Union army in one of the biggest bombardments in American history. With this massive display of strength, Lee hoped to knock out Union cannons so that the field in front of Cemetery Ridge would be clear for attack. The effort turned out to be a waste of ammunition. Lee did not know that he was more or less shooting over the heads of the Union forces. Since the Confederates had overshot, most of the Union artillery was still intact.

After the smoke had cleared, the Union army on Culp Hill watched as a line of Confederate troops began forming on Seminary Ridge. Thinking that the Union cannons had been destroyed, 15,000 Confederate soldiers prepared to attack Cemetery Ridge. In front was Pickett's division, which would lead the charge. Just before the assault Pickett turned to Longstreet and asked, "General, shall I advance?" Longstreet barely nodded.

Pickett leads the charge

Upon receiving Longstreet's order, Pickett mounted his horse and galloped across the valley. Behind him came his 4,300-man regiment, followed by nearly 11,000 other Confederate soldiers. The men moved more than 1,000 yards across the field to Cemetery Ridge. Union officers described the Confederate advance as a "beautiful" sight. Soldiers were marching shoulder to shoulder in half-mile-wide ranks (lines), red Con-

GETTYSBURG REMEMBERED

On November 19, 1863, President Abraham Lincoln dedicated a national cemetery on the battlefield at Gettysburg. Lincoln's address at the site has become one of the most quoted speeches in modern history. The battlefield was later preserved as the Gettysburg National Military Park. Monuments commemorate the site of Pickett's Charge, as well as the other principal conflicts in the Battle of Gettysburg.

federate flags were waving, horses were prancing, and gleaming weapons formed a sea of flashing light. Maintaining perfect formation, the endless ranks of troops moved silently and resolutely as one body over the land—into ditches, over walls, across streams and ridges, through orchards and cornfields.

Before the charge, the Confederates had sensed they might be in trouble, but they did not expect such a strong artillery barrage from the Union side. When the Yankee cannons opened fire, the Confederates were showered with grapeshot (a lethal type of cannon fire). What followed was one of the bloodiest military massacres in history— 6,500 Confederate soldiers were killed or captured. Among the dead were some of Lee's best men, including the veterans who had won a series of victories before the Battle of Gettysburg. A company of students from the University of Mississippi, who called themselves the "University Greys," were all killed or wounded.

The bloodiest battle

Meade did not launch a counterattack after Pickett's advance. There could have been several reasons why Meade did not retaliate. Perhaps he was shocked. Maybe he felt that the slaughter of thousands of men in a short period of time was decisive enough. Possibly he did not attack because he thought that Lee was still dangerous. Whatever Meade's reason for holding back, on July 4, 1863, the Confederate army retreated from Gettysburg with no interference from Union forces. Gettysburg was the worst battle of the war. The South suffered 28,000 casualties (deaths), while the North lost 23,000 men. The effect of the battle on the town of Gettysburg was devastating, as homes were turned into hospitals that became drenched with the blood of thousands of wounded and dying soldiers.

Confederacy doomed

On July 4 Vicksburg was also defeated by the North. The Confederacy had now suffered two crushing defeats in a row. Lee eventually offered to resign, but Davis told him to remain in command. The root of the Gettysburg fiasco lay in Davis's poor judgement. The Confederate leader had been misled by the thought of mounting an offensive campaign (that is, initiating hostilities) in Pennsylvania rather than guarding Vicksburg, an important strategic point. Both Davis and Lee were led astray by visions of larger conquests, thus helping to bring about the downfall of the Confederacy within two years.

FOR FURTHER REFERENCE

Books

Johnson, Neil. *The Battle of Gettysburg.* New York City: Four Winds Press, 1989.

Ward, Geoffrey C., with Ric Burns and Ken Burns. *The Civil War.* New York City: Knopf, 1990, pp. 235–36, 268–69.

Other

The Civil War. [Videocassette] Public Broadcasting Service (PBS-TV), 1990.

The Battle of Little Bighorn

JUNE 25, 1876

George Custer made several mistakes at the Battle of Little Bighorn, but his greatest error was ignoring the advice of other soldiers and his own scouts.

The Battle of Little Bighorn (sometimes referred to as "Custer's Last Stand") is perhaps most famous for being the final campaign of Lieutenant Colonel George Armstrong Custer. The battle is also important, however, because it graphically illustrates the depth of tension between the United States government and Native Americans in the late nineteenth century. The skirmish at Little Bighorn was the result of a dispute over the Dakota Territory (an area that lay west of the Missouri River). This land had long been home to the Sioux and Cheyenne Indians, but white settlers, eager to homestead the region, often ignored the tribes' right to occupy the territory. Custer never really understood how hard the Sioux and the Cheyenne would fight for a place they considered sacred ground; he also underestimated the strength of the tribal leaders' battle strategy. As a result, Custer and his entire regiment were killed.

Impressive but troubled career

Custer began his military career during the Civil War (1861–65; a conflict in the United States between Northern states [or the Union] and eleven Southern states that seceded, or withdrew, from the Union and formed the Confederate States of America [also known as the Confederacy] with U.S. Senator

George Armstrong Custer graduated last in his class at West Point. Despite this dubious distinction, Custer rapidly rose in the ranks of the Union army during the Civil War.

Jefferson Davis as president). Although he graduated last in a class of thirty-four cadets from the United States Military Academy at West Point (New York) in 1861, within two years Custer had become the youngest brigadier general (the rank above colonel) in the Union army. Custer commanded a cavalry brigade in several Union victories over Confederate forces. When the army was reorganized after the Civil War, Custer was given the rank of lieutenant colonel and assigned to command the 7th Cavalry in the western United States.

In 1867 Custer was charged with being absent without permission from his post at Fort Wallace, Kansas. Although he was court-martialed (found guilty by a military court) and removed from his command, Custer was reinstated the next year. When Custer led a massacre of Cheyenne Indian forces at the battle of Washita (Oklahoma) in 1868, he was accused of abandoning some of his own men during the fighting. All of the soldiers were killed.

Territory sacred to Native Americans

In 1873 Custer headed an expedition to the Black Hills in the Dakota Territory, an act that renewed hostilities with the Sioux. Continuing conflicts between settlers and the Sioux—as well as the government's often hostile and contradictory attitude toward Indian affairs—contributed to the tense environment. Before the Little Bighorn battle, Sioux and Cheyenne tribes had control of the Dakota Territory. In the Second Treaty of Fort Laramie (a document signed in 1868), the government promised that these tribes could continue to occupy the territory. Despite the treaty, however, white settlers looking for gold began to move into the region, forcing the Sioux and the Cheyenne further and further off their land.

The tribes protested the presence of the settlers and the violation of the treaty. In response, the U.S. government offered to buy the land. The Indians would not sell, however, because

GEORGE ARMSTRONG CUSTER George Armstrong Custer (1839–1876) was born in New Rumley, Ohio, and graduated from the United States Military Academy at West Point in 1861. He went on to a spectacular career as the youngest brigadier general in the Union army during the Civil War (1861–65). Custer was a handsome man with long blond hair, and his distinguished military record only enhanced his status as a dashing, romantic figure. After the war Custer was placed in command of the 7th Cavalry in the western United States. In 1873 he headed an expedition to the Black Hills in the Dakota Territory, long-time home of the Sioux Indians. In 1874 Custer wrote *My Life on the Plains,* a book that glorified his military achievements. In 1876 continuing conflicts with the Sioux led to the disastrous Battle of Little Bighorn, where Custer and all of his men were killed. Custer's wife, Elizabeth Bacon Custer (1842–1933), devoted her energies to preserving her husband's memory. Among the books she wrote about Custer's life were *Boots and Saddles* (1885), *Tenting on the Plains* (1887), and *Following the Guidon* (1890).

they considered the area sacred ground. Because of a possible gold strike in the area, the government was likewise unwilling to tell the miners and settlers to leave. Government officials finally justified retaliation against the tribes by claiming that they had violated the Second Treaty of Fort Laramie with periodic attacks on white settlers.

Custer is overconfident

In June 1876 the government sent troops led by Brigadier General Alfred H. Terry (1827–1890) to subdue the Sioux and the Cheyenne in the Dakota Territory. Included in the campaign was Custer's 7th Cavalry. The army marched from Bismarck (in present-day North Dakota) to the Yellowstone River. Terry planned to mount the attack in three separate columns (military units). He assigned Custer to command one of the columns, which would move ahead to search for the enemy. Terry instructed Custer to wait for reinforcements if he came upon the Indians, and that under no circumstances should he stage an attack on his own.

On June 25 Custer found the Sioux and Cheyenne in an encampment on the Little Bighorn River in present-day Montana. In direct defiance of Terry's orders, Custer decided to attack. Setting up his own camp nearby, he prepared his troops for battle. Custer made several mistakes at Little Bighorn, but

George Armstrong Custer and the entire 7th Cavalry were killed at the Battle of Little Bighorn.

his greatest error was ignoring the advice of other soldiers and his own scouts. For example, before he left on the campaign Custer was advised to take along Gatling guns (a type of large machine gun). The rapid-firing weapons would have given him a major advantage over the Indians. But Custer had such confidence in the 7th Cavalry that he did not think he needed the extra guns. Then, as the troops were making their camp, Custer's Indian scouts warned the soldiers not to build campfires. The scouts claimed the smoke would be spotted by the enemy. Yet Custer ignored their advice and the Sioux saw the smoke, thus ruining any chance for a surprise attack.

"Custer's Last Stand"

Custer was also tricked by the Sioux and Cheyenne. Although 15,000 people appeared to be in the Indian encamp-

CRAZY HORSE Crazy Horse was a chief of the Oglala Sioux and a prominent leader in the late-nineteenth-century Indian resistance movement. In March 1876 Crazy Horse and the Oglala Sioux refused to go onto a reservation (an area set aside by the government where native tribes were required to live). When the Sioux camp on the Powder River (in present-day Montana) was attacked by the U.S. Army, the Indians staged a victorious defense. The following June, Crazy Horse led another successful battle against U.S. troops at Rosebud creek (also in present-day Montana). Later that month he joined fellow Sioux leaders Chief Sitting Bull and Chief Gall in defeating George Custer at the Little Bighorn.

In January 1877, however, Crazy Horse and about 1,000 Oglala Sioux were reduced to starvation by an army attack. The following May they surrendered to the federal Indian agency in Red Cloud (in present-day Nebraska). Crazy Horse was jailed for allegedly plotting a revolt. As he attempted to escape, he was fatally stabbed in the stomach with a bayonet (a knife-like weapon attached to the end of a gun barrel).

ment, most of the warriors were hidden in ravines (small, steep valleys) along the river. Custer developed a three-pronged plan of attack, sending two units of his regiment—one commanded by Major Marcus Reno and one led by Captain Frederick W. Benteen—to attack the encampment farther upstream. Custer remained with a unit of 211 men that he intended to lead in a direct charge across the river.

Custer had not stopped to consider that, with the Reno and Benteen units several miles away, help would be out of reach. In fact, by the time Custer finally began his charge, the Reno-Benteen regiments were being overwhelmed by Indians. Reno attacked first and had to retreat across the river. Eventually Benteen's troops arrived and continued to hold off the Sioux and Cheyenne. In the meantime, the movement of U.S. troops had alerted the Sioux and Cheyenne that Custer was about to attack, so their main force rode at full speed to his position.

After Custer led his charge, he was surrounded by thousands of warriors under the command of Sioux leaders Chief Crazy Horse (died in 1877), Chief Sitting Bull (c. 1831–1890), and Chief Gall (1840–1894). Pushed back onto a slope, Custer and his men dismounted their horses and tried to fight the Indians on the ground. Within an hour the 7th Cavalry was totally wiped out, except for a lone horse. The Indians stripped and scalped the troops, although they left Custer's head untouched. (Scalping involves cutting the skin and hair from the head of an enemy. Scalps were often kept as a trophies.) According to legend, the Sioux and Cheyenne recognized Custer by his distinctive golden hair and granted him the respect due a valiant warrior. (Some historians contend, however, that Custer cut his hair short before the battle and that the Sioux knew who he was, even without his long hair.)

Crazy Horse was a chief of the Oglala Sioux and a prominent leader in the late-nineteenth-century Indian resistance movement. Together with Chief Sitting Bull and Chief Gall, Crazy Horse defeated the 7th Cavalry at Little Bighorn.

The 7th Calvary soldiers were buried at the site of the Battle of Little Bighorn, which is now a national monument in Montana. Custer's remains were eventually moved to West Point. The Little Bighorn battle—especially the large loss of U.S. troops—caused a great public outcry. In response, a massive force of U.S. soldiers was deployed to the Dakota Territory, and the Sioux and Cheyenne were eventually forced to surrender.

FOR FURTHER REFERENCE

Books

Steele, Philip. *Little Bighorn.* New York City: New Discovery Books, 1992.

Welsh, James. *Killing Custer: The Battle of Little Bighorn and the Fate of the Plains Indians.* New York City: Norton, 1994.

Other

The Battle of Little Bighorn. [Videocassette] Public Broadcasting Service (PBS-TV), 1993.

Geronimo, the Last Renegade: Custer and the 7th Calvary. [Videocassette] Arts & Entertainment Channel (A&E), 1993.

A Good Day to Die: Kill the Indian, Save the Man. [Videocassette] The Discovery Channel, 1993.

Gallipoli Campaign

FEBRUARY 1915 TO JANUARY 1916

More than 8,000 lives were lost due to the ineptness of an inexperienced commander.

The Gallipoli campaign has been called one of the most disastrous battles of World War I (1914–18). The year-long misadventure began in early 1915 with a British expedition to seize the Dardanelles, a strait that connects the Aegean Sea and the Sea of Marmara in Turkey. When the effort failed, Australian, New Zealand, and French forces (the Allies) were called in to join the British at points around the Gallipoli Peninsula. But the operation began to unravel when the Allies failed to coordinate the arrival of navy and army reinforcements. A confused strategy and long delays enabled the Turks to bring in a massive army. The final phase of the campaign was the bungled Allied landing at Suvla Bay on Gallipoli. Under the command of an inexperienced and inept British officer, the operation resulted in a humiliating defeat at the hands of the Turks. After the loss of 8,000 troops, the Allies withdrew from what should have been a simple mission.

Risky venture in Turkey

In February 1915 General Ian Hamilton (1853–1947) headed a British expedition to open a water route to Russia, one of Britain's main allies in World War I. A direct sea passage would be of immense importance to the war effort. The major obstacle, however, was that the British would have to go

WORLD WAR I World War I (1914–18; sometimes referred to as "The Great War") was the largest war in history up to that time. Involving most major and minor world powers, the conflict began when Archduke Francis Ferdinand of Austria-Hungary was assassinated in Sarajevo on June 23, 1914. The assassin was a Serbian nationalist who advocated Serbian independence from Austria-Hungary. The murder ignited a tense political situation that been growing increasingly complex since the late nineteenth century. It resulted in Germany joining Austria-Hungary in an alliance called the Central Powers, which declared war on Russia (an ally of Serbia) and France. The Central Powers were then joined by the Ottoman Empire. (The Ottoman Empire, which included Turkey, was a vast state surrounding the Mediterranean Sea and the Black Sea.)

Russia, France, and Serbia in turn formed an alliance—called the Allies—with Great Britain and Belgium. The Allies were later joined by Japan, Montenegro, and the United States. The war ended when an armistice (a temporary peace agreement) was signed on November 11, 1918. So immense was the suffering and so great were the losses—an estimated ten million dead and twenty million wounded—that the League of Nations was formed in 1919 to prevent future wars. Lingering hostilities erupted again in 1939 with the beginning of World War II.

through the Dardanelles and the Bosporus straits (narrow bodies of water) to reach the Black Sea. This territory was held by Turkey (part of the Ottoman Empire), a powerful ally of Germany. The first phase of the plan involved gaining control of the Dardenelles, an area between European Turkey on the northwest and Asian Turkey on the southeast that connects the Aegean Sea and the Sea of Marmara. Upon taking the Dardenelles, the British would sweep northeast through the Bosporus strait, which joins the Sea of Marmara with the Black Sea. Along the way they would capture Constantinople, the capital of the Ottoman Empire, on the coast of the Sea of Marmara. Once the route to the Black Sea had been secured, the British would force Turkey out of the war.

Allied invasion fails

The campaign fell apart within a month, as the British were driven out of the Dardanelles by the Turks, under the command of German general Otto Liman von Sanders (1855–1929). At this point Hamilton and other British officials realized they would have to launch an Allied operation. Troops from Australia and New Zealand (countries in the British

Empire) would join the British and take up strategic positions around the east coast of the Gallipoli Peninsula, in European Turkey. In the meantime, French forces would occupy the Asian side of the peninsula. Hamilton would be the supreme commander of all the forces.

Allied cooperation was poor, however, with no coordination in deploying navy and army forces. For instance, there was a two-month lag between the time the British first arrived at Gallipoli in February and the landing of Allied troops in April. As a result, the British staged a premature naval attack that could not be supported by the army. By the time Allied reinforcements arrived on April 25, the Turks had increased their army by 600 percent. The Allies were consequently unable to make any important gains as the standoff continued for almost six months.

Suvla Bay plan

By August, the Allies had failed in all of their attempts to achieve a breakthrough. Finally Hamilton developed another strategy: He would stage a new troop landing at Suvla Bay (now Anafarta Bay) on the west coast of the Gallipoli Peninsula. The landing would be a swift operation that included liberating the Australian and New Zealand troops (called the Anzacs), who had been trapped in a cove since April.

The plan was relatively simple. The Allies would land 22,000 men in the IX Corps on a number of beaches with minimal resistance from the Turks. Next they would march inland, take over a semicircle of hills surrounding the bay, and free the Anzacs. After that mission was completed, the IX Corps and the Anzacs would join to attack Sari Bair (hills in the center of the peninsula). The British would then control the Dardanelles, thus allowing British warships to pass through to the Sea of Marmara. Hamilton and his officers predicted that the campaign could easily be accomplished, but everything had to go according to plan. The crucial factor was seizing the hills held by the Turks, so speed and surprise were important.

Aging general chosen

Of critical importance was the landing of IX Corps, the new British reinforcements, at Suvla Bay. Hamilton told Her-

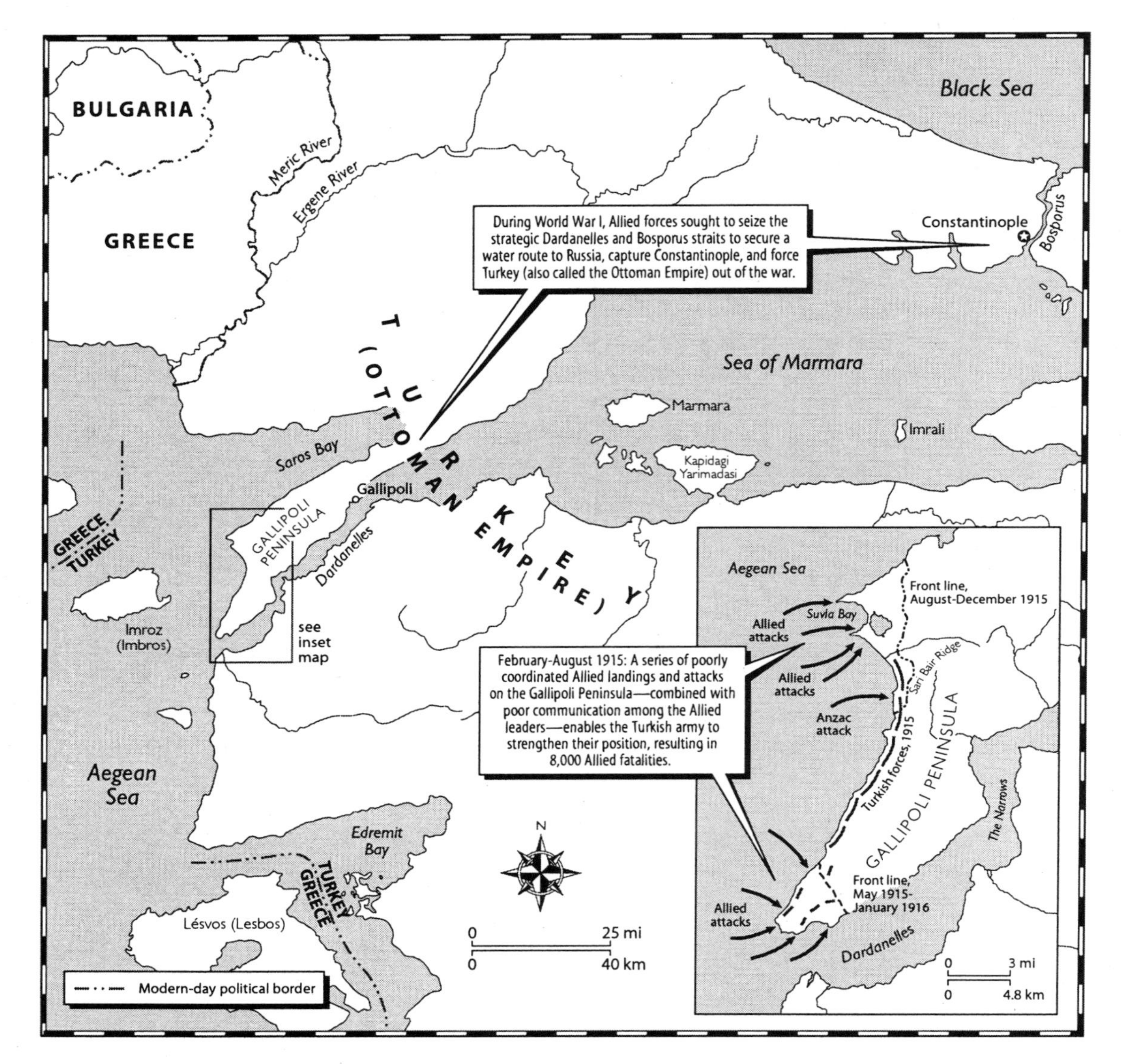

The Gallipoli campaign was hindered by problems from the start, including miscommunication among the Allied forces and poor leadership.

bert Horatio Kitchener (1850–1916), the British war minister, that he needed a competent commander to carry out the mission. Surprisingly, Kitchener assigned a British lieutenant-general named Stopford to head the IX Corps. Although Stopford was a knowledgeable military historian, he had never actually commanded troops. He was also sixty-one years old (and appeared to be even older), so it was unlikely that he could handle the conditions he would face at Gallipoli. Even more puzzling were the officers chosen to accompany Stopford. They, too, were elderly and had been passed up for other duties because of lack of skill or poor health. In fact, one major had just recovered from a nervous breakdown.

Attack stalled

Later in August, Stopford and the IX Corps arrived at Suvla Bay. Stopford, however, did not seem to understand the sense of urgency required for the landing. First, he declared that his men needed to rest for a day, since he felt that getting ashore was a major accomplishment. At that time, there were barely any Turks near the shore to resist the British landing. The attack would have been fast and easy—in fact, the Gallipoli campaign could have been one of the most important victories of the war.

Instead, several officers and their men did virtually nothing when they finally reached shore. The men complained of fatigue and illness as their reasons for staying put. One officer even reported that there were no Turks in his sector, so there was no reason to advance. Another commander decided to throw a tantrum when nine of his twelve brigades (military units) were allocated elsewhere. Because he felt too superior to command such a small group, the commander resigned and refused to attack 700 Turks in the hills with his 3,000 men.

Stopford thwarts victory

Meanwhile, Hamilton was waiting on the island of Imbros (now Imroz; in the Aegean Sea) to hear of Stopford's success. Receiving no reports, he eventually sent two officers to check on IX Corps's progress. The men were astonished by what they found. Stopford was relaxing on his flagship, nursing a painful leg, and had not yet felt well enough to go ashore. The two officers had to restrain themselves from tearing into Stopford for his lackadaisical attitude. British forces had been ashore for almost twenty-four hours and had done nothing except commend themselves for simply achieving a landing. They were missing their chance for a crucial breakthrough. When pressed, Stopford said he would think about advancing the next day.

RUSSELL'S TOP The film *Gallipoli* (1981) portrays the Australian assault against the Turks at Russell's Top on August 7, 1915, during the legendary Gallipoli campaign. Starring Australian actor Mel Gibson, the movie has been praised as a dramatic depiction of the senselessness of war. During the battle at Russell's Top, 600 soldiers of the Australian Light Horse Brigade attacked a hill called Baby 700 in four 150-man waves. The hill was held by the Turks, who had fortified their position with trenches and machine guns. According to the Allied plan, British gunboats along the coast would fire on the Turks as the first wave of men prepared to move. The guns, however, stopped seven minutes early. The Australians did not know what to do, so they decided to wait.

This was a fatal decision because it gave the Turks time to get ready. When the first 150 Australian troops went over the hill they were hit at close range—just 60 yards—by a barrage of bullets. All of the men went down. Although the men in the second wave had witnessed the annihilation of their comrades, they advanced two minutes later and were immediately shot down. As the major in charge of the third wave got ready to follow, he reported to his commander that the effort would be futile. But the commander had heard a false rumor that an Australian flag was flying in the Turkish trenches—indicating that the Australians had taken the enemy stronghold—so he gave the order to advance. The third wave was also wiped out. Although the men in the fourth wave protested that they were facing certain death, they were also sent onto the hill. Casualties were heavy. Of the 435 men who were shot, 232 died.

Stopford then received word that Turkish forces were moving toward Suvla. He casually contacted his divisional commanders to see if they felt like advancing that day. His exact words were: "In view of the want of adequate artillery support, I do not want you to attack an entrenched position held in strength." Given the smallest reason to stay put, the commanders did just that.

Hamilton takes charge

Hamilton decided to visit Suvla himself. When he arrived, Stopford reported that Turkish resistance was too heavy (the Turks had only 1,500 troops, while the British had over ten times that number). He also complained that he did not have enough weapons and that his men were exhausted. Finally, Hamilton ordered one brigade to attack. For some reason, troops occupying a key location, Scimitar Hill, were recalled and ordered to begin digging trenches (long, narrow holes in the ground that give soldiers a safe, concealed place for fighting). With Scimitar Hill abandoned, the Turks simply took over.

The next day Hamilton learned that Stopford had at last decided to go ashore, but his only accomplishment was ordering the construction of a bombproof shelter for his headquarters. By now the Gallipoli campaign was falling apart on all fronts. In one place, 6,000 heavily armed British troops were being held off by 800 Turks who had no machine guns (weapons that can rapidly fire bullets). In another area, an officer told Hamilton that the British were trapped by "one little man with a white beard, one man in a blue coat and one boy in shirt sleeves."

Eventually all the hills on Gallipoli were seized by the Turks. The British had delayed too long. In what could have been a successful mission, Gallipoli was lost because of Stopford's casual attitude. The Suvla Bay landing cost 8,000 British lives. Stopford was dismissed after just nine days in command, and Hamilton was ultimately replaced by Sir Charles Munro. Ironically, historians have noted that the Allies executed a brilliant evacuation on January 9, 1916.

FOR FURTHER REFERENCE

Books

Regan, Geoffrey. *The Book of Military Blunders.* Santa Barbara, CA: ABC-CLIO, 1991, pp. 113–14, 159–61.

The Battle of Verdun

FEBRUARY 1916 TO OCTOBER 1916

The battlefield became a vast open grave.

In February 1916 Germany launched a surprise attack on Verdun, France. The longest engagement of World War I (1914–18), the battle involved more than two million men. The Germans deliberately chose Verdun as the site for their assault because they believed that the French would never retreat from the ancient city. General Erich von Falkenhayn, the German chief of staff, was confident that his massive artillery and elite stormtroopers could "bleed the French to death" by forcing them to use "every man they have." His goal was to eliminate France as an ally of Great Britain, then defeat Britain and win the war.

At first Falkenhayn's plan appeared to be working. His army took the French by surprise and managed to hold the area around the city for several months. The Germans inflicted horrendous damage. Casualties were staggering, Verdun was virtually destroyed, and the countryside was stripped of vegetation by constant shelling. The Germans also used phosphene gas, which penetrated French trenches and killed or disabled thousands of infantrymen. The French ultimately rallied, however, and drove out the German army. Ironically, Falkenhayn—not the French—ran out of men.

Trench warfare

World War I was a revolutionary era in warfare technology. Battles, whether short engagements or long sieges, featured the

Soldiers fighting in the trenches during World War I. Trench warfare was especially brutal, since troops positioned in the narrow, deep ditches were often exposed to poison gas and heavy artillery fire.

extensive use of airplanes, gasoline- and diesel-powered vehicles, automatic weapons, and poison gas. Trench combat, a part of warfare since ancient times, became a vital component of battle strategy. (Trenches are narrow, deep ditches where soldiers conceal themselves from the enemy and fire or launch weapons. Trenches that contain living quarters are called bunkers.) German and Allied forces dug thousands of miles of of trenches that were protected with barbed wire. Since armies tended to stay in one place for long periods of time, the opposing sides had time to try out a variety of weaponry. Armies developed powerful artillery charges (shells and bullets) designed to blow gaps in enemy trenches. Troops also launched trench mortars (tubes through which shells are ejected in a high arc) and tossed hand grenades.

Trench warfare also prompted the development of chemical weapons such as poison gas. Poison gas was first used when the Germans released chlorine gas against the Allies at Ypres, France in 1915. Shortly afterwards, the gas mask (a protective device worn on the face) was introduced as both sides used gas more extensively. The gas shell (a metal casing that contains gas and is launched like a mortar) was introduced by the French.

Other battlefield advances

Another important technological advance was the use of trucks, automobiles, and armored vehicles, which dramatically changed military tactics. Trucks and automobiles could transport troops and supplies more quickly from one battle site to another. Armored vehicles such as tanks could move about the battlefield, protecting the troops inside the vehicle while firing on the enemy and destroying trenches.

Aerial strategy (the use of airplanes in combat) was also heavily employed during World War I. In the beginning of the war, the Germans flew airplanes primarily to spy on the Allies; they later organized small forces of fighter planes for fighting and bombing. The Allies soon followed with their own aircraft. War planes were used for formation flying and the bombing of enemy communication lines, munitions depots (buildings where weapons and ammunition are stored), and trenches.

Verdun besieged by Germans

Verdun was the longest engagement and one of the bloodiest battles of World War I. The Germans set out to wage a definitive battle at Verdun and remove France as an ally of Britain, the main German enemy in the war. The Germans knew that, because of a long history of French-German conflict at Verdun, the French harbored a deep resentment of the Germans and would refuse to retreat from even the fiercest siege.

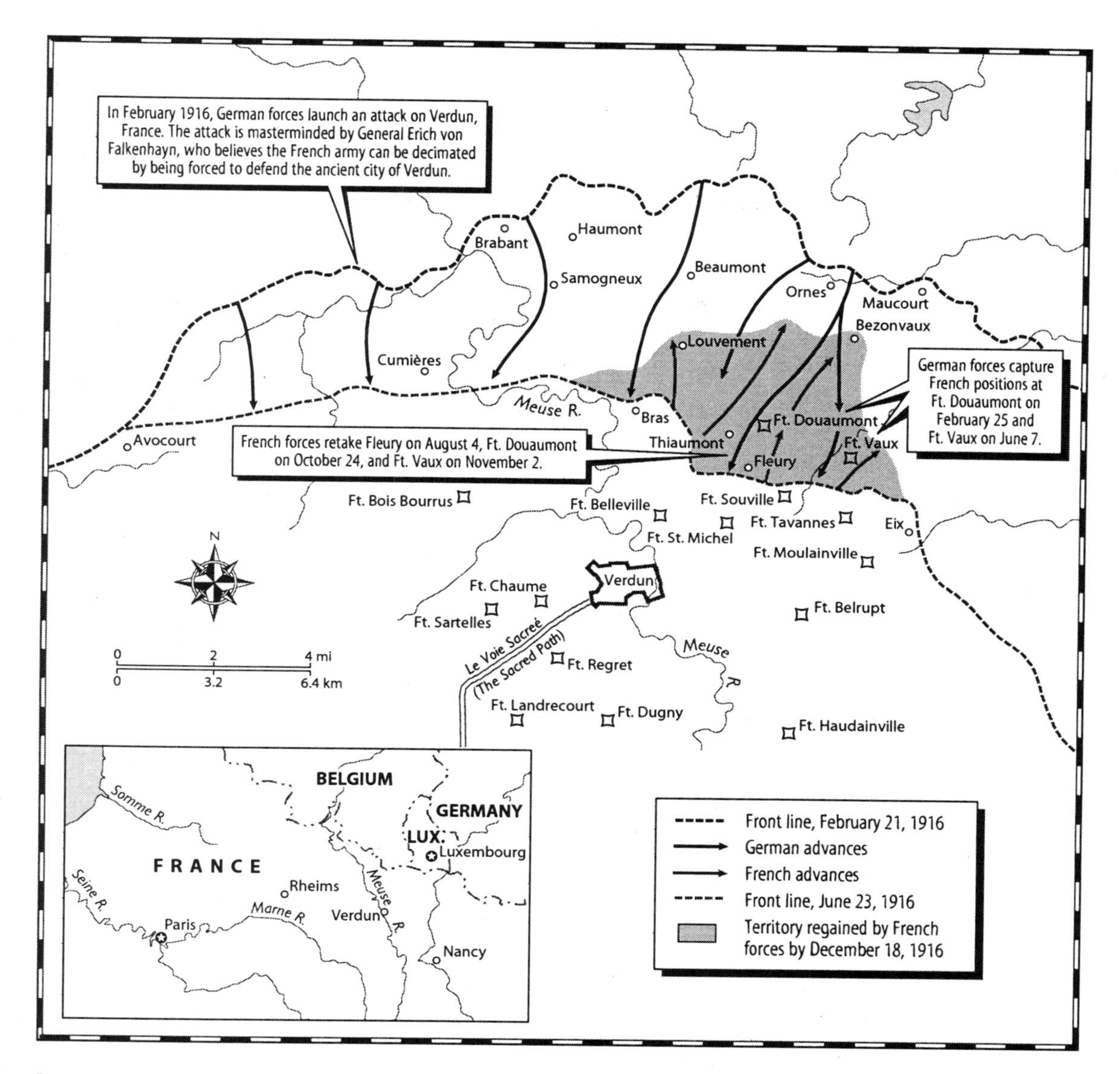

During the Battle of Verdun—the longest engagement in World War I—German forces tried to break the French military line.

Located in the Lorraine region of northwestern France on the Meuse River, Verdun was a Gallic fortress before the Roman era. In A.D. 843 the town was the site of the signing of the Treaty of Verdun, in which the three feuding grandsons of the emperor Charlemagne divided Europe among themselves. Verdun was besieged by Germany at least three times in the centuries before World War I. During the tenth century it was conquered by German invaders, then officially granted back to France in 1648 by the Peace of Westphalia.

During the early years of World War I, Verdun had been untouched by battle. Although the city was surrounded by sixty forts, the French decided to remove all of the weapons so Verdun would not become a German target. In fact, French military commanders reasoned that Verdun was of little strategic value to the Germans because it was 140 miles from Paris (the capital of France). The German commander selected Verdun as the site for Operation "Gericht" ("Execution Place"), however, precisely because it was undefended.

Operation Gericht

The object of Operation Gericht was to drain the French of all their manpower and technological might until there was nothing left. Falkenhayn was certain that once France was broken, Britain would have to beg for peace. In preparation for the Verdun offensive, the Germans secretly positioned massive forces and 1,200 weapons along a front (battle line) eight miles north of the city. Among the soldiers were stormtroopers (members of an elite, private Nazi army), who were known for their aggressiveness and violence. The arsenal consisted of the most advanced artillery (weapons), including "Big Bertha" mortars, flamethrowers, and guns for every purpose, such as firing on the forts, bombarding the town, and shooting at infantrymen. For the Verdun battle the Germans also organized the first "air umbrella." To ward off French planes the Germans would send aloft 168 airplanes, 14 balloons, and 4 zeppelins (lighter-than-air ships).

The French suspected that the Germans were planning an attack, but they assumed the target would be a more strategic location than Verdun. They were finally informed of the Gericht buildup outside the city from refugees (citizens fleeing from the war) and German deserters (soldiers who had left the German army). By this time French military leaders had no time to prepare an adequate defense. The forts around Verdun, no longer stocked with sufficient weapons, were guarded by only a minimum number of troops. Moreover, no other fortifications had been dug on the hills around the city.

Upon learning of the impending German assault, the French commanding officer, General Joseph Joffre, rushed two divisions (large, self-contained units of soldiers, weapons, and supporting equipment) of reinforcements to Verdun and immediately ordered fortifications (walls and trenches) to be constructed along the Meuse River. Just as Falkenhayn and his field commander, Crown Prince Wilhelm, were preparing to attack on February 12, however, a severe blizzard swept in from the hills. The Germans postponed action for eight days while visibility was at zero and snow blanketed the ground. The French waited for the onslaught.

French unprepared

The weather finally cleared on February 19. The longest battle—and one of the most massive bombardments—of World War I commenced the following morning. The Germans unleashed a barrage of shells on Verdun, within hours inflicting heavy damage on the city and reducing the surrounding forests to mere stubble. In an area measuring less than one square mile, eighty thousand shells fell. The human toll was even more devastating. A nine-hour barrage killed one man every five minutes. A company of French chasseurs (elite infantrymen) at the center of the fighting lost more than half of its men in the first day of fighting. Within four days the Germans had advanced swiftly, taking Fort Douaumont and Fort Hardaumont with hardly any opposition from the French. They easily occupied the villages around Verdun.

The fall of Douaumont was a particularly low point in the initial phase of the battle. The giant fort, which had been designed to repel the Germans' "Big Bertha" mortar shells, was a major component in the system of fortifications around Verdun. Usually 500 men were stationed at Douaumont, but at the beginning of the war Joffre had sent them to fight in other battles. When the assault on Verdun began, a single gun turret (tower) was in operation and only fifty-seven gunners were manning the fort. On February 25, a small German unit led by a twenty-four-year-old soldier entered Douaumont through a tunnel. The men took the French totally by surprise, capturing all fifty-seven occupants without a shot. A later analysis of the battle estimated that this ridiculously simple takeover cost the French 100,000 casualties.

Pétain raises morale

Fortunes turned for the French when French general Philipe General Henri Pétain was placed in charge of the defense

of Verdun. Crying "They shall not pass!" the French rallied around their new commander and staged an effective resistance. Pétain's first task was to bring in reinforcements. Although the Germans controlled all rail routes into Verdun, Pétain managed to find a narrow road forty miles to the south. With careful planning and organization, he turned the road into a secure passageway for trucks driven by French volunteers. As vehicles sped by every fourteen seconds, engineers filled holes in the road with gravel and sand. This heroic effort resulted in bringing 200,000 men and 25,000 tons of supplies into Verdun. Pétain's road has since been called *La Voie Sacreé* ("The Sacred Way").

Battlefield a pit of horror

The Germans were startled by the strength and fortitude of the French. The battle continued to rage through May, but the Germans no longer dominated the fighting. They virtually traded the territory back and forth with the French in a series of attacks and counterattacks. In fact, the engagement at Verdun had turned into a horrible, agonizing stalemate. On-the-scene observers said the battlefield looked like an open grave. There was no longer any sign of humanity—just shells exploding onto piles of blasted bodies and battle debris. Strategy had long since been abandoned, so fighting was taking place over and over again in the muck and mud on the same ground, with no gains on either side.

Both the Germans and the French had the most technologically advanced weaponry in history. Yet commanders in each army still relied on the nineteenth-century infantry charge, sending lines of soldiers forward to shoot at the enemy and engage in hand-to-hand combat. Consequently, as stormtroopers and chasseurs swarmed out of their trenches onto the field, they were either blown to bits by artillery fire or they struggled to the death with their opponents. The battle was taking a terrible toll, especially on the Germans, who kept their soldiers at the front until they were mortally wounded or killed. Pétain, on the hand, rotated his troops by withdrawing weary fighters and bringing in fresh recruits.

◀ **In 1932 the Charnel House was built at Verdun in memory of the fierce fighting in the area during World War I.**

GERMANY BUILT "DEATH STRIP" During World War I, Germany introduced various forms of unconventional warfare. Among them was a 112-mile-long electrified "death strip" between German-occupied Belgium and the Netherlands. Built in 1914, the fence stretched from Vaals, Netherlands, to Brugge, Belgium, on the North Sea. The purpose was to prevent spies from crossing into Belgium and to stop smuggling from both sides of the border. Using massive amounts of energy, the 2000-volt fence received electrical power from factories and petroleum generators in the area. At least 3,000 people were killed on the fence (the Germans later disposed of the bodies); many others were captured and hanged.

Many people devised clever ways to avoid being detected or electrocuted. Some pole-vaulted over the barrier, while others jammed empty barrels into the fence and then crawled through to the opposite side. The existence of the death strip was widely disputed until 1998. Then Alex Vanneste, a scholar at the University of Antwerp, discovered proof in documents and photographs. Parts of the fence and a memorial to death strip victims have also been discovered along the border.

Germans make last stand

The third phase of the battle began in June. Falkenhayn had replaced Crown Prince Wilhelm with General Schmidt von Knobelsdorf, who was to stage another major assault called "May Cup." Wilhlem argued against the plan, saying too many lives would be lost. On the French side, Pétain had also been replaced because he, like Wilhelm, refused to launch an offensive. Pétain's successor was General Robert Nivelle, who claimed to have a formula for ending the war.

On June 1 the Germans opened May Cup by again attacking the hills along the Meuse River. A particularly fierce confrontation took place inside tunnels under Fort Vaux, which stood outside Verdun. As German and French soldiers fired machine guns, pistols, grenades, and flame throwers in the narrow tunnels, men smothered to death and bodies decomposed in the intense heat. French troops at Vaux sent out a carrier pigeon with the message "Relief is imperative." The pigeon died upon arriving in Verdun and was later awarded the Legion of Honor. After holding the fort for a week, the French were finally forced to surrender. The Germans moved on to Fort Souville, the last obstacle to Verdun, where they introduced their latest weapon.

"Green Cross Gas"

The battle of Verdun is remembered not only for horrible destruction, but also for the deadliest chemical weapon perfected by either side: a phosphene gas called "Green Cross Gas." The Germans had been working on this chemical weapon for several months. Unlike chlorine and other types of chemical agents previously used in the war, phosphene was fatal, but its victims exhibited no exposure symptoms (such as vomiting. It was called "Green Cross Gas" because the Germans put it in shells painted with bright green crosses.) On June 23 the Germans started firing the shells into the French trenches. The effects were highly lethal (deadly). French troops who seemed perfectly healthy—even those wearing gas masks—were dead within hours. "Green Cross Gas" gave the Germans their first real advantage in months, and they were able to advance within three miles of Verdun. Yet the French managed to regroup and fortify the city with trenches and barricades. Consequently, the poison gas assault amounted to a final and futile effort on the part of the Germans.

Commander runs out of men

On July 1, British and French troops attacked German forces on the Somme River, which empties into the English Channel about 140 miles northwest of Verdun. The battle of the Somme, which involved very heavy fighting, drew German strength away from Verdun. Although the Germans again assaulted Verdun nine days later, they realized that Operation Gericht was a failure: Falkenhayn, who had confidently announced that he would fight the French until their last man fell, had himself run out of men. Over the next two months the French drove the Germans from the area, regaining Fort Douaumont and Fort Vaux. When the fighting ceased at the end of the year, the French had won back all the forts and territory they had lost earlier. But the human losses on both sides were devastating. According to some estimates the combined number of German and French casualties was 420,000 men. Others place the figure even higher, at about 348,000 for the French and 328,000 for the Germans—a total of 676,000.

Verdun was almost totally destroyed by the constant shelling, but it was later rebuilt. Among the numerous monuments now standing in the countryside around Verdun are the Ossuaire de Douaumont and the Monument de la Victoire. More than seventy Allied and German cemeteries are also located in the area. In addition to the monuments and cemeteries, several war museums have been established in the city.

FOR FURTHER REFERENCE

Periodicals

Morris, Roy, Jr. "Nature Herself Murdered." *Military History.* August 1986, pp. 26–33.

The Easter Rising

APRIL 24, 1916, TO APRIL 29, 1916

Disorganization and lapses in communication turned the rebellion into a tragic misadventure.

The Easter Rising (also known as the Easter Rebellion) was a failed insurrection against British rule staged in Dublin, Ireland, on Easter Monday, 1916. The insurgents (people who revolt against the government in power) knew from the outset that their cause was doomed. Yet they hoped that by sacrificing their lives for Irish freedom, they could rally the general populace to take up arms and drive the British out of Ireland. As a result of disorganization and lapses in communication, however, the rebellion turned into a tragic misadventure. Fewer than 2,000 nationalist troops joined in the Dublin rising, and there was virtually no activity in the rest of the country. Hostilities between the rebels and the British army raged for nearly a week, finally halting when the nationalists surrendered on April 29.

Five hundred people—most of them civilians—were killed and 2,500 were wounded during the rebellion. Initially, Irish citizens were outraged at the insurgents for causing needless death and destruction. Then the British executed fifteen of the rebel leaders without a trial, and popular sentiment dramatically shifted toward the nationalist cause. The misguided dreamers became romantic heroes who gave impetus to a renewed nationalist movement, a drive that has continued to the present day.

Padriac Pearse commanded Irish forces during the Easter rebellion. He was later executed by a firing squad for his role in the insurrection.

Roots of the Rising

The Easter Rising was the culmination of centuries of discontent that had been simmering in Ireland since the British first occupied the country in 1171. At various times throughout history, independence groups had staged failed rebellions. By 1914 politicians had won Home Rule for Ireland (that is, Ireland would have its own parliament, but would remain within the British Empire). Home Rule was suspended, however, during World War I (1914–18), thus triggering divided loyalties. Many Irish citizens supported the British war effort. Although Irish men were not conscripted (required to serve in the military) to fight against Germany, some joined the British army. Hundreds of Irish men refused to fight, however, and many even enlisted in the German forces.

British intercept plans

Irish nationalist leaders (people who wanted Ireland to be an independent nation) seized the war as a perfect opportunity to stage a successful revolution. They reasoned that the British would be using all their military strength against Germany and would therefore be left vulnerable to attack on Irish soil. In 1914 nationalists prepared for a conflict with pro-British forces in Ulster (a region that includes the six counties in present-day Northern Ireland). The group managed to smuggle a shipment of illegal German rifles into Dublin. Their contact in Germany was Roger Casement (1864–1916), an Irish-born revolutionary. Although Casement had been knighted (officially honored and given the title of Sir by the British king) for his career as a British agent and humanitarian in Africa, he opposed the British presence in Ireland.

By January 1916 Casement was negotiating with the Germans for arms and soldiers to support a full-fledged rebellion. He was also trying to organize a brigade (military group) among Irish prisoners of war in Germany to fight in the insurrection. The British learned about the plot when they intercepted a coded telegraph message from Germany to Ireland. Unaware of British intelligence activities, the Germans agreed to land arms at Tralee in County Kerry (in southwest Ireland) on April 19. On April 9 the German ship *Aud* was on its way to Tralee with a load of rifles. Two days later Casement—without a brigade or German soldiers—was also bound for Ireland on a German U-19 (submarine). British war ships were following close behind. The insurrection was in trouble.

A change in plans

The plan was also unraveling in Dublin. Like previous Irish rebellions, the Easter Rising was plagued from the outset by poor organization and lack of communication. The rebels belonged to a number of groups. At the center was the Citizen Army, an association of Dublin workers who campaigned for better housing and improved working conditions. They were joined by the Irish Volunteers (a group that sought independence for Ireland), the Irish Republican Brotherhood (IRB; an older organization that formed the core of the Volunteers), and the Sinn Féin party ("we, ourselves" in the Irish language; a small group that advocated guerilla warfare against Britain).

The rebels formed a leadership committee called the IRB Military Council, which included Padriac Pearse (1879–1916), Thomas Clarke (died in 1916), Joseph Plunkett (died in 1916), James Connolly (1868–1916), Sean MacDermott (died in 1916), Eamonn Ceannt (died in 1916), and Eoin MacNeill (died in 1945). After lengthy meetings and discussions the council decided to hold a Volunteers' parade in Dublin at noon on Easter Day, April 23. Using the parade as a cover, the revolutionaries would seize strategically located buildings, then declare Ireland a free and independent republic. The following day Volunteers would mobilize throughout Ireland and be supplied with German guns. Joining forces with the Irish brigade and German soldiers, the rebels would then take over the country.

Lapses in communication, internal squabbling

The problem was that the Military Council had originally set delivery of the guns for April 19. When they moved the date of the rising to April 23, the council sent a message to Ger-

PADRIAC PEARSE Padriac Henry Pearse (1879–1916) was the motivating force behind the Easter Rising. Born in Dublin, he was the elder son and second of four children of James Pearse, an English stonecarver, and Margaret Pearse, a shop clerk. As a child, Padriac Pearse was influenced by an aunt who taught him patriotic ballads and tales based on Irish mythology and history. After learning the Gaelic (Irish) language while he was a teenager, Pearse formed an intensely romantic view of Ireland. He also became an inspirational public speaker.

Although Pearse studied law, he turned to teaching when his father died and he had to support the family. In 1908 he founded St. Enda's secondary school for boys, where he taught Gaelic and promoted a distinctly Irish culture. Pearse extended his political activity in 1913 when he joined the Irish Volunteers, a group that sought independence from Britain. He commanded Irish forces during the failed Easter Rising of 1916. For his role in the insurrection, Pearse was executed by firing squad on May 3, 1916. The best known of the fifteen executed rebels, Pearse has become a mythic figure among Irish nationalists.

man headquarters in Berlin, requesting arms and reinforcements no earlier than April 24. But the *Aud,* which was already on its way, did not have a radio and there was no way to relay the message. Unaware of this disastrous development, the rebel leaders proceeded with their preparations. Soon the organization broke down because of internal conflict. Pearse, Clarke, and others on the Military Council wanted to use force when staging the insurrection. MacNeill, the Volunteers' commander in chief, insisted that his men should fire their weapons only to defend themselves. Pearse and Clarke therefore forged a document that outlined supposed British plans to round up the Volunteers during the parade. They intended to show the document to MacNeill shortly before the rebellion to persuade him to take offensive action. Pearse and Clarke were also formulating military strategy with Volunteers in other parts of Ireland without MacNeill's knowledge.

Guns not delivered

On April 19 the *Aud* reached the Kerry coast but no one arrived to meet the ship. Lieutenant Karl Spindler, the commander, kept the *Aud* in the water off Tralee harbor for several hours. When no signal came from the shore and British warships began closing in, Spindler headed the *Aud* back out to sea. After the ship was intercepted by the British, Spindler blew it up (along with the guns) to prevent it from being captured. In the meantime, as the submarine chugged toward Ireland, Casement was frantic. The Germans had supplied only a small number of outdated rifles and no soldiers. Moreover, there was no Irish brigade; Casement simply hoped he could reach Ireland in time to call off the rebellion.

Around midnight on April 20 the U-19 arrived at Tralee. The *Aud,* which was supposed to meet the submarine, was nowhere in sight. The U-19 captain took his submarine up to the surface of the water, dropped Casement on shore, and turned back toward Germany. Within hours Casement was arrested. On Saturday, April 22, MacNeill learned that Casement was in British custody and the *Aud* had been scuttled (blown up). That night MacNeill canceled the parade—and the rising. The following morning he ran a coded announcement in the *Sunday Independent* newspaper, alerting Volunteers throughout the country to the change in plans. Just hours before the rising was supposed to take place, the Military Council held a heated debate and decided to reschedule it for Easter Monday. Then all council members except MacNeill signed a proclamation of independence, which had been written by Pearse.

Rising begins

The rising commenced at noon on Easter Monday, without MacNeill (he joined the fighting later in the day). Pearse commanded the rebel troops in a futile attempt to attack Dublin Castle, the seat of British government. Then the main insurgent force—headed by Pearse, Connolly, Clarke, and MacDermott—established headquarters in the Dublin General Post Office (GPO). As a massive audience looked on, Pearse read the Proclamation aloud and ordered that it be posted throughout the city. Other rebel units had taken positions in the Four Courts (government buildings), St. Stephen's Green (a park), the South Dublin Union (the offices of a labor organization), Jacob's Factory (a bakery), and Boland's Mill. Later they took over the College of Surgeons (a medical facility).

An independent Irish government was also formed, with Clarke as president. As a result of mixed signals, however, fewer than 2,000 men ultimately showed up to take part in the Dublin rising. In the rest of Ireland, Volunteers had become confused by the change in orders, and outbreaks occurred only in isolated

Irish-born revolutionary Roger Casement had been knighted by the English king for his career as a British agent and humanitarian in Africa.

places. The rebels did not receive the popular support they had anticipated. Most citizens considered them to be a nuisance at best, and at worst a threat to national security.

Success, then surrender

British officials had been caught off guard by the rising, even though they had been monitoring IRB Military Council activity. Initially, the rebels had surprising success. They managed to maintain all of their strongholds, and they inflicted heavy casualties on the British army. One famous battle involved a regiment called the Sherwood Foresters that was marching into the city from Dún Laoghaire (an area on the coast, south of Dublin). The rebels concealed themselves in rowhouses in a residential area near Boland's Mill, then shot the British soldiers with sniper fire.

During a week of constant street fighting, bombardment, and fires, downtown Dublin was devastated. Looting of shops and stores was rampant, especially among the poor, who—dodging bullets—poured out of tenements (rundown rental housing) to swoop up candy and baked goods, pull on layers of clothing, and cart away furniture. As citizens went about their daily routine, they stopped to watch the fighting or taunt the rebels. Many innocent people, however, were caught in the crossfire. Eventually the rebels were worn down. The British moved the gunboat *Helga* into the River Liffey, which flows through the center of the city, and bombarded the GPO. Shortly thereafter, on Saturday, April 29, Pearse, Connolly, and MacDermott surrendered the rebel forces. The men claimed to have made the move to prevent further killing of civilians. (In actuality they were outnumbered and had been hemmed in, with no means of escape.)

Rebels executed

By the end of hostilities 500 people had been killed and 2,500 wounded, the majority of them civilians. Sixty rebels

THE TRAGIC FATE OF MICHAEL COLLINS

One of the most famous Irish revolutionaries was Michael Collins (1890–1922). Nicknamed "Big Fella," Collins was born in West Cork, Ireland, and spent his early adult years (1907 to 1916) in England. During that time he joined the Fenians, a radical political group devoted to ending British rule in Ireland. In the Easter Rising of 1916 Collins served in Padriac Pearse's unit, which took over the General Post Office. In 1919, as a member of the Sinn Féin nationalist movement, he helped form the Dáil Eireann (a revolutionary government). That year he also organized the IRA guerilla campaign (nontraditional warfare that involves ambush) against British rule, ultimately forcing the British to seek a truce.

In 1921 Collins was instrumental in negotiating the treaty that established the Irish Free State. Under the terms of the agreement, Ireland would have its own parliament (governing body), but it would remain a part of the British Commonwealth. Although Collins had not obtained complete independence for Ireland, he realized it was the only settlement England would accept at the time. He served as finance minister in the new government under president Arthur Griffith (1872–1922). In 1922 Collins was assassinated by extremists who were dissatisfied with the treaty and wanted total freedom from Britain.

The film *Michael Collins* (1996) traces the last six years of Collins's life. Starring actor Liam Neeson in the title role, the story begins with the surrender of the Easter Rising rebels and depicts the events leading up to the formation of the Irish Free State. The screenplay emphasizes the conflict among the revolutionaries, particularly between Collins and Eamon de Valera, over the terms of the Free State treaty.

and 132 soldiers and policemen also died. After the surrender more than 2,000 people were detained by British authorities, although many had not participated in the rebellion. Ninety prisoners were sentenced to death in a secret court-martial (military trial) headed by British general John Maxwell. In spite of pleas for clemency (leniency) from Irish and British officials, Maxwell ordered the execution by firing squad of fifteen rebel leaders between May 3 and May 12. The signers of the Proclamation were all put to death.

The rebels met their fate heroically, but the final moments of Plunkett and Connolly were particularly poignant. Just a few days before the rising, Plunkett had had surgery and during the siege he lay as a virtual invalid in the GPO. He was executed in spite of his condition. During the fighting Connolly sustained a leg wound that had become gangrenous (soft tissue had died due to loss of blood). Since he could not walk or stand, the British carried him on a chair and placed him in front of the fir-

Eamon de Valera, commander of the Boland's Mill detachment, was sentenced to life imprisonment for his role in the Easter Rising.

ing squad. Casement's story was equally tragic. After the rising, in which he did not participate, he was taken to England and imprisoned in the Tower of London. As his health deteriorated, he became nearly blind and tried to commit suicide. Casement was hanged in August 1916.

The lives of many other rebel leaders were spared. MacNeill was sentenced to life in prison. Constance Markiewicz (1868–1927), an Anglo-Irish aristocrat who commanded the unit on St. Stephen's Green, was scheduled to be executed. At the last minute, however, the British refused to put her to death because of her gender—much to the disappointment of Markiewicz, who wanted to die for her country. Eamon de Valera (1882–1975), commander of the detachment at Boland's Mill, also received a death sentence. Probably because he was an American citizen, his sentence was later reduced to penal servitude (hard labor) for life. Following an international outcry over the ruthless executions, many of the participants of the rising were given life in prison.

Continued violence

Maxwell had intended the executions to be a lesson to the Irish that Britain rule could not be challenged illegally. During the rising the majority of citizens shared this view. But the mood of the country soon shifted. Disturbed that the revolutionaries had been put to death without a trial or even the right to retain lawyers, the Irish quickly turned toward the nationalist cause. Although the independent government had collapsed when the rebel leaders were arrested, the British were never able to regain a dominant political position in Ireland. In fact, the 1916 Easter Rising was the beginning of the end of British rule in the twenty-six counties that eventually became the present-day Republic of Ireland.

On December 6, 1921, the Irish Free State was established as an independent entity within the British Commonwealth.

But dissension and internal squabbling marred this first chance for independence when a year-long civil war broke out in 1922. Led by de Valera and others, nationalists established a revolutionary government and fought against the Irish state for total freedom from Britain. The Republic of Ireland was finally established in 1937, and de Valera was elected the first president of the new nation. Under this arrangement the twenty-six predominantly Roman Catholic counties in the south and west became an independent country. Northern Ireland (six mainly Protestant counties in Ulster) remained under British rule.

This division led to even more violence in the 1970s as the Irish Republican Army (IRA) guerilla campaign escalated in Northern Ireland. Known as "the troubles," the bloody conflict soon involved other paramilitary groups (fighting forces organized on a military pattern) and continued into the 1990s. An international commission was appointed to resolve religious, political, and social differences among the various factions. Although the IRA declared two formal cease-fires, isolated bombings and killings were reported. By 1998 more than 3,000 people had died in the fighting.

FOR FURTHER REFERENCE

Books

De Rosa, Peter. *Rebels*. Dublin, Ireland: Poolbeg Press, 1996.

The Amritsar Massacre

APRIL 13, 1919

The Amritsar Massacre helped give rise to the Indian independence movement led by Mohandas Gandhi.

On April 13, 1919, British troops fired without warning upon a crowd of protesters in Amritsar, India, killing an estimated 379 people and wounding 1,200 others. The incident, later known as the Amritsar Massacre, was initiated by Brigadier General Reginald E.H. Dyer, largely in response to a mob attack on a female English missionary. The shooting was followed by a proclamation of martial (military) law, public floggings (whippings), and other measures aimed at humiliating the Indian people. Word of the incident and Dyer's actions was received with horror in England. The Hunter Commission was established to investigate Dyer, who was later condemned and relieved of his post. The Amritsar Massacre helped give rise to the Indian independence movement led by Mohandas Gandhi. Over time, the movement helped create the free state of India.

Dyer sent to Amritsar

After World War I (1914–18), the people of India were still working to gain independence from British rule. In Amritsar (the largest city in the Punjab state, in northwestern India on the border of Pakistan), violence was breaking out in the streets. A British missionary named Miss Sherwood was beaten and murdered by an Indian mob. Brigadier General Reginald E.H. Dyer (1864–1927) was immediately sent to restore order.

AMRITSAR Amritsar was founded in 1577 by Ran Das, the fourth Guru of the Sikhs (the Sikhs are followers of a religion that combines aspects of Hinduism and Islam and teaches the existence of one god). The city was built around a sacred pool called Amrita Saras, from which the word "amritsar" was derived. A temple was built on an island in the center of the tank. After its dome was covered in gold foil, the temple was named *Harimandir* ("Golden Temple"). The temple eventually became the center of the Sikh faith. Because of Amritsar's central location, trade increased and the city became a part of British India in 1849.

Amritsar was the site of two political clashes that resulted in the deaths of many people. The first, the Amritsar Massacre, took place at Jallianwalla Bagh, a park in the city where a national monument now stands. The second occurred in 1984, when the Indian army attacked Sikhs who were fortified in and around the Golden Temple. Some reports indicated that 450 people died in the incident, while others placed the death toll at 1,200.

A quick-tempered man who suffered from arteriosclerosis (hardening of the arteries), Dyer was filled with rage toward the Indian people when he received word of Sherwood's death.

Proclamation ignored by activists

Dyer arrived in Amritsar with 1,000 British, Indian, and Gurkha troops (soldiers from Nepal, a country on the northeast border of India). The British deputy commissioner (city official) had issued a proclamation that groups of four or more Indians would be fired upon. The proclamation was read throughout the city, but had little effect on Indian activists (people who promote social and political change), who mocked its message and demanded that the British leave the country. Dyer received additional orders from the viceroy (a governor who represents the king) that troops should be used to show that the British would not tolerate defiance from Indians.

In the meantime, Indians deliberately ignored the message by calling a meeting on April 13, 1919, at the Jallianwalla Bagh, a park of about an acre surrounded by houses and walls. Thousands of people who were unafraid of British threats gathered to hear speeches. Infuriated by this obvious act of defiance, the lieutenant governor of Punjab placed Amritsar under martial law. Dyer was sent to deal with the crowds at Jallianwalla Bagh, and the day ended in disaster.

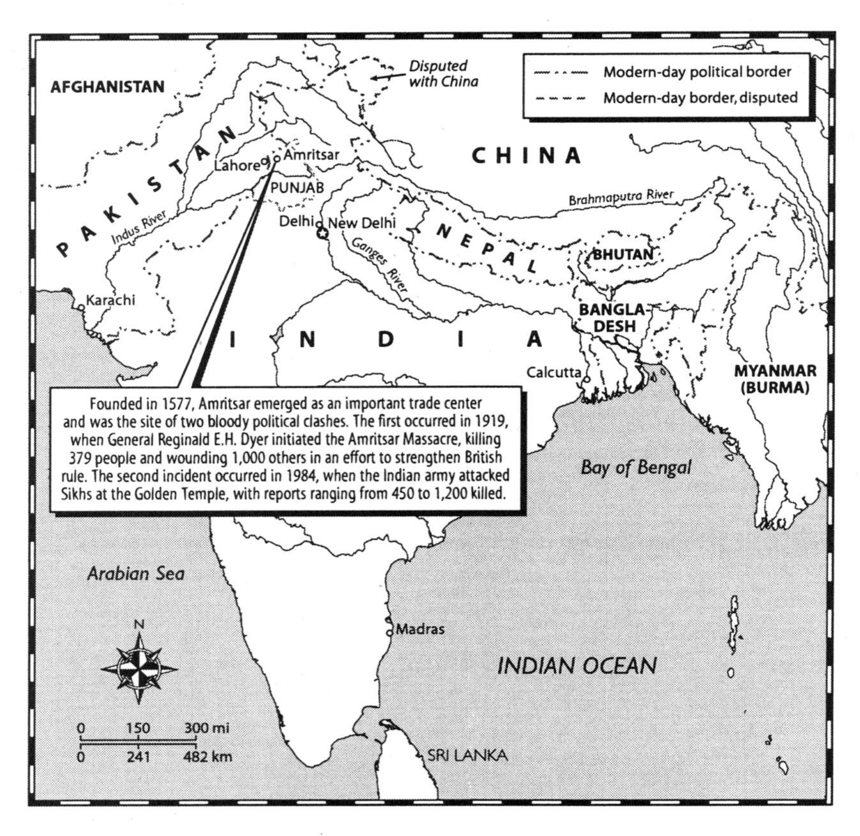

The Amritsar Massacre influenced Indian activists to fight for their country's independence from British rule.

British open fire at Jallianwalla Bagh

Dyer led twenty-five Sikhs (members of an Indian religious group), sixty-five Gurkhas (only half of whom had rifles), and two armored cars to the location. The cars were left behind because they would not fit through the entrance to the park. As the small army marched straight into the arena, Dyer ordered his troops to open fire. The protestors were shocked, and someone even yelled, "They are only blanks!" This hopeful statement was met with bloodshed. Frantically, people searched for a way out, but the crowd was blocked by Dyer's men. The only escape route was the way Dyer and his men had used to enter Jallianwalla Bagh.

The soldiers randomly fired their guns, felling hundreds of Indians. When the troops ran out of ammunition, they reloaded their rifles and kept on shooting. Altogether, the sol-

MOHANDAS GANDHI

Mohandas Gandhi (also called Mahatma; 1869–1948), an Indian nationalist and spiritual leader, is widely regarded as the father of his country. Gandhi became a political activist in 1893 after visiting South Africa to investigate the mistreatment of Indian immigrants by whites. In 1906 he started the *Satyagraha* ("firmness in truth") campaign, which championed passive resistance to, and noncooperation with, government in order to achieve political goals. Gandhi went on to work against British rule in India, eventually founding the campaign for Indian independence. He was imprisoned several times, and in 1932 he staged a "fast unto death" (a hunger strike) as a protest against British treatment of "untouchables" (the lowest class in Indian society). Over the years, however, the independence movement moved beyond Ghandi's control and he became less active (although he helped negotiate terms for an independent Indian state in 1947). In 1948 Gandhi was assassinated by a fanatical Hindu (an intensely devoted follower of Hinduism, the dominant religion in India). Gandhi's methods of nonviolent civil disobedience have been adopted by civil rights and political activists throughout the world.

diers used 1,650 rounds of bullets. Three hundred seventy-nine people were killed, and one thousand were wounded. (Dyer later claimed that he and his men saw no women and children in the park, but this is very unlikely.) Showing no compassion, the British did not lift a finger to help the victims. They simply marched out the way they had come in. Dyer expressed no doubt or remorse over his decision, and the lieutenant governor immediately endorsed his actions. In fact, Dyer was considered a hero.

Cruel and outrageous measures

After the massacre, Dyer inflicted widespread punishment on the Indian population. He demanded that all methods of Indian transportation, including bicycles and carts, be confiscated (taken away). Dyer required Indian lawyers to work as coolies (unskilled laborers); he also forced them to view public floggings.

Dyer's prejudice eventually drove him to institute even more outlandish measures. He ordered Indians to salaam (a salutation shown by bowing very low and placing the right palm on the forehead) when meeting Europeans. Out of respect to the fallen Miss Sherwood, he decreed that anyone who crossed the lane where she had been attacked must do so

Mohandas Gandhi was an Indian nationalist and the spiritual leader of the Indian independence movement. Gandhi advocated nonviolent civil disobedience as an instrument of change.

on their hands and knees—any refusal was met with flogging. Soon the floggings spread all over Punjab. For instance, the members of a wedding party in one town were whipped for breaking curfew (a regulation requiring certain people to be off the streets at a specified time). The situation was no longer an effort to restore civility, but instead a cruel show of power by a deranged man.

Dyer denounced, then made rich

The British government in England finally reacted to Dyer's misuse of authority. Voicing the shock and horror of British citizens, Winston Churchill (1874–1965) denounced Dyer for initiating the Amritsar massacre and humiliating the Indians. An investigative body called the Hunter Commission then issued a report that condemned Dyer for ordering his troops to use all their ammunition on an unsuspecting crowd. Dyer was relieved of his post and ordered to return to England.

In a move that many people found appalling, the House of Lords applauded Dyer's actions. (The House of Lords is one of the two governing bodies in the British Parliament; members of the House of Lords represent the upper classes, while members of the House of Commons represent the middle and working classes.) In an even more outrageous development, supporters in the House of Lords started a benefit fund for Dyer that later made the soldier a wealthy man.

Catalyst for Indian independence

The Amritsar Massacre and the subsequent endorsement of Dyer by the British aristocracy only solidified Indian opinion that there could never be equality between the races. According to Indian activists, the only answer was political independence. The massacre eventually gave rise to the teachings of Mohandas Gandhi (1869–1948), who headed the movement that gained independence for India in 1949.

FOR FURTHER REFERENCE

Books

Faber, Doris, and Harold Faber. *Mahatma Gandhi.* New York City: J. Messner, 1986.

Operation Barbarossa

1941 TO 1942

When Hitler was forced to withdraw his forces in March 1942, the German army had been reduced by almost one-third.

In 1941, in the midst of World War II (1939–45), German leader Adolf Hitler devised a plan to invade the former Soviet Union. As part of his invasion scheme, Hitler organized a massive military campaign code-named "Operation Barbarossa." Despite huge military and personnel backing, however, Operation Barbarossa eventually failed. There were a number of reasons for this failure. Hitler underestimated the size, strength, and determination of the Russian Red Army; he also insisted on controlling many aspects of the invasion personally, removing all of the generals who disagreed with him and making himself the head of the German army. Unfortunately, Hitler knew very little about military strategy and his battle plans did not take into account the Russian winter. The extremely cold Soviet climate exacted a terrible toll on German troops, who were unaccustomed to the bitter weather. When Hitler was finally forced to withdraw his forces in March 1942, the German army had been reduced by almost one-third.

Hitler plans to invade Russia

Since the 1920s Hitler had wanted to acquire new territory for Germany. He thought the country was too small to accommodate a growing population, that the German people needed *Lebensraum* ("room to live"). Hitler's opportunity for expansion came at the beginning of World War II. By the summer of 1940, when France surrendered to the Nazis, German armies had conquered most of Europe in a series of overwhelming victories. Yet Britain, which had a powerful air force and navy, remained at war with Germany. British fighter planes defeated Hitler's Luftwaffe (air force) at the Battle of Britain (July to October 1940). After gaining air superiority, Britain used its navy to prevent German forces from crossing the English Channel (a body of water between Britain and France) from France to invade Britain. Germany therefore could not move into Britain, but neither could Britain invade Nazi-controlled Europe.

Adolf Hitler's decision to personally lead Operation Barbarossa proved disastrous for German troops.

Although Germany and Britain continued the war, most of Hitler's army was not involved. Hitler had decided to use his forces to pursue *Lebensraum* in eastern Europe. In order to achieve this goal, Germany would need to conquer White Russia (present-day Belarus, a country that borders Poland) and Ukraine. Both countries had long been part of the Russian empire, but in 1917 they were incorporated into the Union of Soviet Socialist Republics (U.S.S.R.; usually called the Soviet Union) after Communists overthrew the Russian monarchy. (Communism is a political and economic theory that advocates the formation of a classless society through communal, or group, ownership of all property.) The Soviet Union had also acquired the eastern half of Poland in 1939 as part of a nonaggression treaty with Hitler (sometimes called the Nazi-Soviet Pact), just before Germany conquered the western half of the country.

Invasion supports Nazi racial theory

Shortly after forming the agreement, Hitler began to feel threatened by the Soviet Union, which he had always distrusted because of his hatred of communism. The Soviets had taken over Lithuania, Latvia, and Estonia (three small countries on the shores of the Baltic Sea), which Hitler wanted for Germany. The Soviet move strengthened Hitler's resolve to invade Russia.

ADOLF HITLER Adolf Hitler (1889–1945) was born in Upper Austria. After serving in World War I, he joined the National Socialist German Workers' party (the Nazi party). In 1921 he became president of the organization and established a private army of storm troopers called the "Sturmabteilung" (also referred to as the "SA"). Two years later Hitler led an unsuccessful government revolt called the "Beer Hall Putsch." For his part in the revolt, Hitler was sentenced to prison for five years (he was paroled after nine months). While he was in prison Hitler began dictating *Mein Kampf* to his secretary Rudolf Hess (1894–1987). The book later became infamous as a statement of Nazi racist and totalitarian philosophy (advocacy of German racial superiority and absolute rule by a small group of leaders).

By 1933 Hitler had rebuilt the Nazi party and was named chancellor (chief minister of state) of Germany. He used his power to capitalize on German nationalism and growing economic uncertainty. (Nationalism is an intense loyalty to one's country.) A year later he dissolved the army, combined the offices of chancellor and president, and gave himself the title "Der Fürhrer" ("supreme leader"). With a number of loyal associates Hitler initiated a reign of terror based on the concept of Germans as members of a superior race. Beginning in the early 1930s Hitler set up a system of concentration camps for the extermination of millions of Jews and political enemies.

Hitler's invasion of Poland in 1939 helped start World War II, a conflict that ultimately involved most of the countries of the world. The German leader achieved military successes early in the war, but failures in Russia, Africa, and Italy soon dealt a severe blow to Hitler's plans for expanding German territories in eastern Europe. As the Germans continued to lose the war, Hitler increasingly retreated from public view. During this time he escaped several assassination attempts. Hitler committed suicide on April 30, 1945, shortly before the Russians occupied Berlin (the capital of Germany).

His goals were also heavily influenced by the Nazi belief that Germans were members of a superior race. According to the Nazi view, this special status gave Germans the right to occupy eastern Europe and use the "inferior" inhabitants—Poles, Russians, Ukrainians, White Russians, and others—as sources of cheap labor.

Another crucial factor in Hitler's plan of conquest was an intense hatred and fear of Jews. The Nazis felt that the Jews were gaining too much power in German lands. Since the western Soviet Union (which included eastern Poland) was the home of five million Jews, it posed an especially urgent threat. Moreover, the Nazis believed the Jews were plotting with the Communists to take over the world. Thus the German invasion

German army trucks head down the Minsk-Moscow highway on July 18, 1941.

of the Soviet Union became a mission not only to acquire new territory but also to destroy communism and to annihilate (wipe out completely) the Jews.

Operation Barbarossa launched

After a series of delays Hitler and his generals set the invasion of the Soviet Union for June 1941. Operation Barbarossa was to be a massive campaign. (In fact, some historians have called Operation Barbarossa the most powerful invasion force of all time.) For their assault the Germans assembled one hundred and fifty divisions with a total of three million men. There were 3,000 panzers (a special type of German tank) in 19 divisions, 7,000 artillery (weapons) pieces, and 2,500 Luftwaffe fighter planes and bombers. (A division is a self-contained military unit that is capable of independent action.) The Germans had also recruited thirty divisions of Finnish and Romanian troops. Hitler planned to take all of Russia (the European part of the Soviet Union) and part of the Ukraine (a country in the

On October 2, 1941, German troops arrived at Czarskoie Selo, a castle near Leningrad formally used by the czars and their families.

western Soviet Union bordering on Poland and Hungary). The German forces expected to defeat the Red Army (the name given to the Soviet army) within two or three months, so they were confident their troops would be back in Germany before the Russian winter set in.

On June 22, 1941, the Germans moved into Russia and the Ukraine along an 1,800-mile front (line of battle). They took the Soviets completely by surprise, catching the Red Army unprepared. Within five days German forces had captured the city of Minsk (the capital of Belarus) and had taken 300,000 prisoners. Yet many Soviet troops were able to escape to the east, eventually blocking roads and impeding the Germans' progress. Hitler's army continued the eastward advance and, on July 14, occupied the city of Smolensk (on the Dnieper River in western Russia), taking 200,000 Soviet prisoners. Again Soviet forces staged a strong resistance. Nevertheless, the Germans succeeded in occupying most of European Russia and overrunning Red Army forces. Germany's domination to this point was primarily the result of its famous mechanized divisions (panzers and other armored vehicles). But Hitler's troops were soon confronted with a serious problem: bad weather. Within days rainstorms had turned sandy roads into thick mud that trapped tanks and transport vehicles.

Russians fight back

At this point the Russians started fighting back with a "scorched earth" strategy. To ensure that the Germans had nothing to conquer, the Soviets burned crops, blew up bridges, destroyed railroads, and evacuated factories. They even dismantled steel and weapons plants in the west and shipped them by rail to the east. The factories were quickly rebuilt and put back into production. In spite of these obstacles, the Germans advanced eastward more than 400 miles and were within only 200 miles of Moscow (the largest city in the Soviet Union). Their prospects of occupying Moscow and winning the war seemed to be highly favorable.

In August, however, cracks began to appear in Operation Barbarossa when Hitler and his generals had a disagreement about their next move. They found that, in spite of the size of the German campaign, the Soviet Union had two to three times the number of tanks and aircraft as the Germans. The Germans still had one advantage, however, for the Soviet air force was outmoded and consisted of inferior fighter planes and bombers.

The German intelligence service (spy network) had also underestimated the number of Soviet troops. By August the Red Army had brought in more than 200 fresh divisions, making a total of 360. Consequently, as soon as the Germans defeated one Soviet army they instantly ran into thousands of reinforcements. These miscalculations caused Hitler and his advisers to waste most of the month of August arguing about strategy. The generals wanted to concentrate on seizing Moscow, but Hitler was determined to expand the war. He finally decided to send more forces into the Ukraine and Caucasia (also called Caucasus; a region south of the Ukraine between the Black and Caspian seas). He then gave orders to take Leningrad (the second largest city in the Soviet Union).

For a time, the Germans continued to defeat Soviet army attempts to regroup. By the end of September they had encircled Red Army forces near Kiev (a city in the Ukraine), captur-

Adolf Hitler began his invasion of the Soviet Union—an assault called Operation Barbarossa—in June 1941.

ing 520,000 men. The Soviets had become vulnerable because of poor leadership and differences of opinion among military commanders.

Invasion thwarted by cold

With winter approaching, Hitler stopped the drive into Leningrad and gave orders to move on to Moscow instead. The invasion of Moscow, under the command of Field Marshall Fedor von Bock (1880–1945), began on October 2, 1941. At first victory seemed assured. German forces had just captured 600,000 more Soviet troops, thus clearing a route into the city. But by November the German soldiers were extremely weary, travel was nearly impossible, and casualties were mounting. Because the soldiers did not have adequate clothing for the severe climate, they suffered from frostbite. Moreover, German trucks, tanks, artillery, and aircraft had become paralyzed in the ice and snow. By November 730,000 Germans had died. The Soviets, on the other hand, were accustomed to the climate and wore heavy clothing that enabled them to fight in cold weather. Thus they gained a significant tactical advantage.

Hitler takes control

On November 22 German forces under General Paul von Kleist (1881–1954) nearly reached the Caucasia, but ran out of fuel for their tanks at Rostov-on-Don (a city in southwest Russia). Commander in chief Karl von Rundstedt (1875–1953) surveyed the situation and proposed that the army evacuate the area. He was overruled by Hitler. On November 26 the Soviets moved in and occupied Rostov. Four days later Hitler relieved Rundstedt of command and appointed himself commander in chief. The Germans plodded onward, encountering more Soviet forces. Several German generals suggested setting up a winter camp, but Bock wanted to continue the advance toward Moscow. He was sure the Soviets could easily be overcome, a view that was shared by Hitler. On December 2, a few German forces managed to go into the suburbs of Moscow, but most of the army remained in the forests around the city. Instead of staging a definitive victory in the assault on Moscow, the German army was gradually being defeated by the most severe Russian winter in several decades.

The Soviets took advantage of the Germans' vulnerability and launched a series of counterattacks. During this time Hitler continued to overrule his generals, dismissing those who did not agree with him, including Bock. He also declared war on the United States on December 11, 1941. (On December 7, 1941, Japan—Germany's ally in World War II—had bombed Pearl Harbor; the next day the United States declared war on Japan.) Although Hitler had no experience

THE ARMY TANK Military attack and defense tactics were revolutionized during World War I (1914–18) by mechanized warfare, or machines powered by gasoline and diesel engines. In addition to the airplane, the most important innovation was the tank. The tank is a vehicle covered with heavy metal that has caterpillar traction (it moves on two endless metal belts called tracks) and is armed with machine guns, cannon, rockets, or flamethrowers. Developed by Great Britain, the tank was first used successfully in the British surprise attack on German forces at Cambrai, France, in 1917. In World War II tanks became an integral part of warfare. Germany won the opening engagement of the war in 1939 by conquering Poland in less than a month with armies of tanks (armored units) called panzers.

Soon the tank was being used by both sides, and often the outcome of a battle depended on which army most effectively deployed armored units. As the war progressed, tanks were designed for various functions, such as amphibious landings (carrying troops and supplies from ships to land) and clearing mines (explosive devices buried in the ground). Tank warfare gave rise to specialized weapons, including bazookas (firing tubes that launch tank-piercing rockets), antitank missiles, and aircraft armed with bombs and rockets. The basic technology of a tank remains unchanged today, although the machines are now equipped with laser target detectors, computerized navigation systems, and specialized armor.

as a military leader, throughout the campaign he had taken charge of plotting strategies, giving orders to generals, and planning bombing raids. As he assumed more control, Hitler continued to reject intelligence reports and relied on his own estimates of enemy equipment strength and troop movements. Months of planning had gone into Operation Barbarossa, but by now Hitler had thrown aside the work of experienced generals and other advisers. Consequently the Germany army was again put at a tactical disadvantage while having to endure the cruel climate.

Barbarossa fails

Throughout the winter of 1941–42, as sub-zero temperatures plunged even lower, the German army came under repeated Soviet assault. Especially damaging were strikes by Siberian troops, who were superb fighters in cold weather. (These troops came from Siberia in the northernmost part of the Soviet Union, on the Arctic Ocean.) In spite of this emergency Hitler would not approve a full-scale retreat, so his troops were subjected to continued suffering.

The Red Army campaign lasted for more than three months, and by March 1942 the Soviets had made several important gains. Nevertheless, the Germans managed to hold onto isolated towns around Moscow that they occupied during their defensive campaign. Before the winter ended, however, much of the German army had been depleted to only one-third of its original strength. The Luftwaffe had also been drained by carrying supplies under severe weather conditions to the remote towns where the Germans were stationed.

Hitler finally agreed to withdraw from the Soviet Union, but the disastrous decisions he made during the campaign were to have lasting effects on the German army. It was never fully rebuilt. An even more critical outcome resulted from Hitler's having broken the nonaggression treaty with the Soviet Union. In July 1941, shortly after Hitler launched Operation Barbarossa, the Soviet Union entered World War II as an ally of Great Britain and the United States. The Allies went on to defeat Germany, Japan, and Italy (known as the Axis Powers) in 1945.

FOR FURTHER REFERENCE

Books

Feldman, George. *Understanding the Holocaust.* Detroit: U•X•L, 1998, pp. 177–211.

Wepman, Dennis. *Adolf Hitler.* New York City: Chelsea House, 1985.

Kamikaze at Leyte Gulf

OCTOBER 21 TO OCTOBER 26, 1944

Japan's loss at Leyte Gulf exposed the samurai tradition as being tragically out of place in modern warfare.

During World War II (1939–45), Japan became famous for its kamikaze air force, a corp of young suicide fliers. In the tradition of Japanese samurai warriors, kamikaze pilots crashed their planes into Allied ships in order to inflict heavy damage. The flyers took pride in this act because they were sacrificing their lives for their country. The first extensive kamikaze attack was staged at the battle of Leyte Gulf in the Philippines in 1944. Some historians have described the engagement as a full-scale kamikaze assault because it involved not only the suicide fliers, but also the rest of Japan's air force and even the navy. The operation was a disaster for Japan, however, because Allied forces destroyed nearly half of the Japanese fleet. In spite of its sweeping all-or-nothing effort, Japan succeeded in sinking only a few American ships. A crucial turning point in the war, the Leyte Gulf battle exposed the samurai tradition as being tragically out of place in modern technological warfare.

Japan enters war

When World War II started in Europe in 1939, Japan signed a military pact with Germany and Italy (countries in the Axis Powers), who were fighting Great Britain, France, and Albania (countries in the Allied forces). Japan sent troops into

Indochina (the southeast peninsula of Asia), where it was vying for power with China. Then Japan set out to create and lead the Greater East Asia Co-Prosperity Sphere (a union of countries in Southeast Asia), an act that was opposed by the United States. In October 1941, General Hideki Tojo (1884–1948) became prime minister of Japan. (The Japanese prime minister is head of the diet, the equivalent of a parliament).

As the military gained total control in Japan, the United States continued to criticize the country's activities in Southeast Asia. In retaliation, Japan decided to initiate hostilities against the United States. On December 7, 1941, the Japanese air force staged a surprise attack on the U.S. Pacific Fleet at Pearl Harbor, an American naval base on the island of Oahu, Hawaii. The same day Japan also struck Allied bases at Singapore (a British possession on the Malay Peninsula) and elsewhere in the Pacific Ocean. On December 8 the United States joined the Allies and declared war on Japan, thus escalating the conflict to involve most of the major world powers. (The Soviet Union had recently joined the Allies after being invaded by Germany.)

The kamikaze

For over a year Japan expanded its military might throughout the Pacific and into India and Alaska. Japanese leaders attributed this success to their samurai warrior heritage, a tradition of duty and honor that dated back to the twelfth century and formed the basis of the nation's military code. Kamikaze suicide pilots were an important part of Japan's strategy in the war. The pilots took their name from a typhoon, or whirlwind, called the *Kamikaze* ("divine wind"). Kamikaze fliers were the most aggressive component of the air force, which coordinated its assault tactics with the Japanese navy. Regular pilots used their fighter planes as an umbrella by firing upon a target (usually a ship) from the air to protect battleships (the largest and most heavily armed warships) and destroyers (small, fast warships with guns, torpedoes, and other weapons). At the same time the battleships and destroyers launched an artillery assault. Then suicide bombers would make a quick, direct strike that destroyed the target.

The aircraft used by kamikaze pilots were usually light bombers or fighter planes that were loaded with bombs and extra gasoline. A piloted missile—called a "Betty bomber" by

A stricken kamikaze plane falls toward the ocean after being hit during battle in the western Pacific Ocean on April 20, 1945.

the Japanese and nicknamed "Baka" (the Japanese word for "fool") by Allied soldiers—was also developed for use by the suicide fliers. Equipped with three rocket engines and containing a ton of explosives in its nose, the missile was attached to a plane. The kamikaze pilot launched the missile from an altitude of 25,000 feet about 50 miles away from the target. The missile would glide for about 47 miles before the pilot turned on the rocket engines, which would accelerate to over 600 miles an hour. Going into the final dive, the pilot would crash into the target. Since there was no way for the pilot to get out of the plane, he died on impact.

Suicide missions a last resort

From 1941 to 1942, Japanese commanders had great success with their coordinated air and naval strategy as they conquered islands in the Pacific. The Philippine Islands served as the main line of defense between the Allies and Japan. The Japanese were sure they could hold this line. Japanese commanders also believed that they would soon wipe out Allied forces and achieve a decisive victory. By 1944, however, the war was requiring more pilots than Japan was able to train. Prior to this time, air force and navy commanders had maintained rigid entrance requirements for flying schools. Faced with an ever-increasing demand for flyers, however, the military began expanding enrollment on a monthly basis, accepting any man who could be taught to fly and shoot straight. Consequently, many Japanese pilots were no longer superior to their American counterparts.

The main problem was that Japan could not keep pace with technologically superior American planes and aircraft carriers (ships that serve as a base for warplanes in the ocean or sea). Most of these craft were equipped with antiaircraft weapons. These weapons had become especially effective in shooting down kamikaze before they were able to crash into ships. Yet, as more and more Japanese planes were destroyed by these sophisticated war machines, Japan began to rely even more heavily on kamikaze suicide missions to sink U.S. ships. This strategy simply worsened an already serious situation, as valuable pilots were lost in attacks that often failed. Once the mighty aggressor, Japan was forced into a defensive position to protect its territory in the Pacific and to keep the war from reaching Japan itself.

The *Sho* I campaign

In 1942 the Allies gradually began taking back the islands Japan had conquered in the Pacific. By 1944 the Americans were preparing to invade the Philippines. To prevent an invasion, Admiral Soemu Toyoda, commander in chief of the Japanese

THE SAMURAI The kamikaze pilots of World War II were part of the samurai tradition. The samurai were a warrior class that arose during Japan's feudal period. Feudalism—usually associated with Western European countries—was characterized by a rigid social class structure, and land was owned by the upper class, or aristocracy. All other classes were controlled by the aristocracy through a complex system that required them to pay fees, perform certain duties, and show respect. In Japan the system was adopted around the tenth century. From the twelfth century onward, the samurai were the dominant upper class. Japan was ruled by samurai military governors called shoguns until the Meiji restoration (1867-68), a revolution during which shoguns were replaced by the emperor.

Samurai warriors wore two swords that they were entitled to use on any commoner (member of a lower class) who offended them. The samurai adhered to the bushido, a strict honor code developed around 1185 and written down in the sixteenth century. The bushido required indifference to pain or death, loyalty to one's superiors, and self-sacrifice. The samurai shunned business and profit motives (acquiring wealth by selling goods and services). After the Meiji restoration, bushido was taught in state schools by former shoguns and was mandatory for all government officials and employees. Former samurai were instrumental in building modern Japan. Bushido was the basis for emperor worship, which continued until Japan was defeated in World War II. During the war Japanese military commanders conducted battle strategy according to bushido principles, and kamikaze pilots dedicated themselves to this honor code.

Combined Fleet, developed a plan called *Sho* I. The plan was designed to hold onto the Philippines and protect the Japanese oil supply route to East India. According to Toyoda's strategy, on October 22, 1944, Japanese battleships, along with supporting destroyers and other ships, would set out for the Philippines. Under the command of Vice Admiral Kurita, the fleet would converge on the islands of Samar, Luzon, Leyte, and Minanoa.

Sho I called for the Japanese navy to trap the U.S. Third Fleet and Seventh Fleet in a surprise attack. Supporting this ambitious campaign would be Japanese air and naval forces based in the Philippines, which were commanded by Vice Admiral Shigeru Fukudome. To implement *Sho* I, Japanese commanders had to hit the Americans hard and sink as many ships as possible. Since the Japanese air force had recently been weakened and pilots and planes were in short supply, Fukudome was to use his planes only to provide an umbrella for the attacking battleships. He was specifically ordered not to engage in any kamikaze raids. Although the Japanese did not expect to win a total victory in the Philippines, they hoped to delay an American invasion by inflicting significant damage on the U.S. Navy and Air Force. Thus Japan would gain some extra time to fortify defenses along its shores. But in order for *Sho* I to work, most of the Japanese ships and planes would have to be sacrificed. Commanders, pilots, and sailors all knew the plan amounted to a huge kamikaze-like operation, but they were willing to take the risk.

The battle of Leyte Gulf

Sho I was completely doomed because the Americans were aware of the plan from the start. Unknown to Japan, the U.S. military in the Pacific had been monitoring communications about the plan through a code-interception system called SIGINT, or "signal intercept." Since the Americans were able to prepare for the Japanese arrival in the Philippines, the element of surprise was eliminated. As early as October 17, the Japanese knew U.S. ships were heading toward Leyte Island (a landmass between Luzon on the north and Mindanoa on the south), but they decided *Sho* I should commence anyway. Three days later General Douglas MacArthur (1880–1964; see "Military" entry), supreme commander of U.S. forces in the Pacific, began landing 738 ships and 132,000 Allied troops at Leyte. He was assisted by the Seventh Fleet under Admiral Thomas Kinkaid (1888–1972). On October 23, Japan's main force, led by Vice Admiral Kurita, approached Palwan Island in the Philippines. The battle of Leyte Gulf (a body of water on the east coast of Leyte) was soon under way.

Once again the Japanese had been outwitted by superior technology. The Americans had tracked the movement of the Japanese ships and planes with radar (*ra*dio *d*etecting *a*nd *r*anging). As Kurita's fleet entered the waters near the Philippines, it was immediately attacked by two U.S. submarines. Several cruisers (large, fast gunboats) were damaged and two ships were sunk, including Kurita's own *Atago*. Kurita was rescued from the sea and transferred to the *Yamato*, which was at that time the world's biggest battleship. As the Japanese entered the Sibuyan Sea (a small body of water in the center of a cluster of islands south of Luzon) the next morning, the *Yamato* and its fleet came under heavy bombardment from U.S. warships. According to *Sho* I, Kurita was to have the protection of

Dead Japanese kamikaze pilots lie by the ruins of their bomber after an attack in Okinawa on May 24, 1945.

Fukudome's air force at this critical moment. But Fukudome and his planes were nowhere in sight.

Fukudome disobeys orders

In fact, the Japanese air force had been nearly wiped out. As the planes were passing over Luzon Island (the chief and northernmost island in the Philippines) on October 21, they encountered an intense blaze of U.S. antiaircraft fire. In response, Fukudome disobeyed orders and told his pilots to make kamikaze strikes on the enemy. This led to the largest kamikaze assault of the war. Although the 200 Japanese planes succeeded in sinking the U.S. aircraft carrier *Princeton,* nearly all of the aircraft were destroyed or lost. In the meantime, Kurita's ships had to proceed without an air umbrella as they tried to fend off hundreds of American planes. One of the battleships, the supposedly unsinkable *Mushashi,* went down with almost all of her crew in the San Bernardino Strait (the main entrance to the Philippines, southeast of Luzon).

With four battleships remaining, Kurita regrouped as night began to fall. The following morning, October 25, he managed to gain an advantage because the Americans thought they had totally destroyed his fleet in the Sibuyan Sea. Then two other phases of *Sho* I were put into effect. According to the plan, ships commanded by Vice Admiral Jisaburo Ozawa would first come in from the north as a decoy (a tactic to divert attention elsewhere). The ships were to draw the U.S. Third Fleet under Admiral William F. Halsey (1882–1959) away from the center of conflict. In spite of the fact that SIGINT had revealed Ozawa's ships were a decoy, Halsey fell for the trick and went after them.

In the second phase, a Japanese fleet under Vice Admiral Nishimura was heading into the area to join Kurita. Kurita and Nishimura would then strike the Seventh Fleet. But *Sho* I failed again. As Nishimura's forces moved toward Leyte Gulf from the south, they were met by a fifteen-mile line of U.S. ships. Although the barrier could not be penetrated, Nishimura drove his fleet straight into destroyers, PT boats (*p*atrol *t*orpedo boats), and torpedo boats. He and his crew went down in flames with his battleship as the rest of the fleet were nearly annihilated.

Defeat at Leyte Gulf

While U.S. forces were being engaged by Osawa and Nishimura, Kurita was moving toward Leyte Gulf. He had easily navigated the *Yamato* and the rest of the fleet 150 miles past the San Bernardino Strait. Then he accidentally encountered eighteen U.S. aircraft carriers commanded by Admiral Thomas Sprague. Sprague was not prepared to engage the Japanese, especially the monstrous *Yamato*. Although he put out several SOS ("Save our ship") distress signals, Sprague got no reinforcements. In desperation he sent up his 378 fighter planes, which fired on the Japanese ships.

At this point *Sho* I completely fell apart because Kurita mistakenly assumed Sprague was heavily reinforced. Apparently panicking, Kurita gave an order for a "general attack" (this meant that ship commanders were on their own). There was no strategy or battle line, so for the next few hours the Japanese assaulted Sprague's carriers at random. They managed to sink three U.S. ships before losing two of their own. Kurita could not seem to decide whether to continue on to Leyte Island. Finally, he gave up and retreated toward the San Bernardino

Strait. Meanwhile, to the north, Ozawa's fleet had been almost completely destroyed in a massive ten-hour bombardment by Halsey's forces. The Japanese had lost one of the largest naval engagements in history.

Japan surrenders

The self-destructive gamble at Leyte Gulf was a disaster for Japan. By October 26, forty percent of the Japanese combined fleet had been wiped out. On the other hand, American losses were light—only 2.8 percent of the combined fleet was lost. Nevertheless, the Japanese managed to revitalize their forces. A few months later, on April 1, 1945, they staged a last bloody naval confrontation with the United States at Okinawa, Japan. In that battle the kamikaze inflicted the greatest losses ever suffered by the U.S. Navy in a single campaign—almost 5,000 men were killed. Despite this victory, the Japanese met their final defeat shortly after Okinawa. The following August, the United States dropped atomic bombs on the cities of Hiroshima and Nagasaki. Japan surrendered on August 14 and signed a formal treaty on September 2.

FOR FURTHER READING

Books

Naito, Hatsuho. *Thundergods: The Kamikaze Pilots Tell Their Story.* New York City: Kodansha International, 1989.

General Douglas MacArthur in Korea

1950 TO 1951

"Old soldiers never die; they just fade away."

—Douglas MacArthur

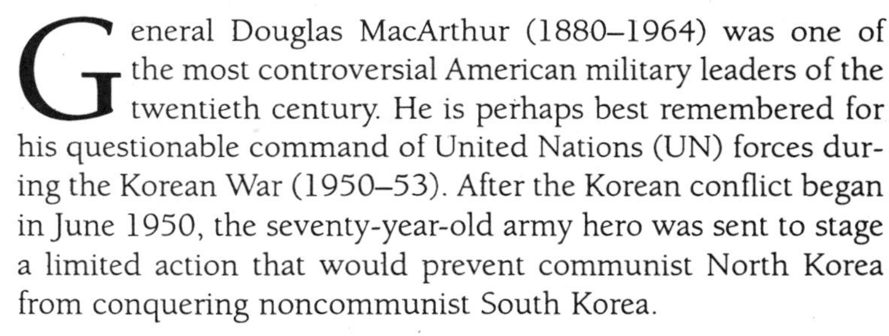

General Douglas MacArthur (1880–1964) was one of the most controversial American military leaders of the twentieth century. He is perhaps best remembered for his questionable command of United Nations (UN) forces during the Korean War (1950–53). After the Korean conflict began in June 1950, the seventy-year-old army hero was sent to stage a limited action that would prevent communist North Korea from conquering noncommunist South Korea.

Yet MacArthur had a mission of his own as he crossed the 38th parallel (the invisible line dividing the two parts of the country)—he wanted to wipe out communism. In order to achieve this goal, MacArthur advocated extreme measures, including the use of atom bombs against China (Korea's communist neighbor to the north). As UN losses mounted, President Harry S Truman (1884–1972) began questioning the general's behavior. Finally, on April 11, 1951, Truman relieved MacArthur of his commands, charging him with insubordination (refusal to obey orders).

MacArthur heads UN troops in Korea

Following World War II (1939–45), Korea was divided into two separate zones of occupation at the 38th parallel. The Union of Soviet Socialist Republics (the Soviet Union) occu-

In 1950 seventy-year-old general Douglas MacArthur assumed command of the United Nations' forces in Korea.

pied the north and the United States occupied the south. In 1948 two opposing governments were created—the democratic Republic of Korea (South Korea) and the communist People's Democratic Republic of Korea (North Korea). Political strains developed over the next two years, and on June 25, 1950, North Korea invaded South Korea. The UN (an international organization dedicated to world peace and security) immediately declared the invasion to be an act of aggression. Demanding withdrawal of North Korean troops, the UN called on member nations to support South Korea. Within two weeks the United States and fifteen other UN nations were preparing to send troops to Korea to help resolve the conflict. President Truman appointed MacArthur as supreme commander of the joint forces.

Although MacArthur was seventy years old, he seemed to be the ideal choice for leading a military engagement in Asia. During World War II he had commanded U.S. forces in the Southwest Pacific, and at the time of the Korean conflict, he was still head of the Allied occupation of Japan (the process of using American and British troops to make the transition from war to peace). He was also the U.S. Army commander in the Far East (Asia). MacArthur was therefore a seasoned veteran in Asia—in fact, he had not set foot on American soil since 1941, when he left retirement to return to active service.

Inchon invasion succeeds

By the time MacArthur arrived in Korea on July 8, North Korean troops had overwhelmed the South Korean army. MacArthur immediately requested more men and equipment. At the end of July he had 45,000 U.S. ground troops under his command, and within four weeks the number had risen to 150,000. Nevertheless, North Korea still managed to drive American units and the South Korean army all the way down to Pusan, on the southeast tip of Korea. On September 15,

THE BILLY MITCHELL CASE

General Douglas MacArthur had a role in the famous Billy Mitchell case. General William "Billy" Mitchell (1879–1936) was an American army officer and pilot who advocated the use of air power in warfare. He supported using airplanes to carry out bomb strikes and actively campaigned for the creation of an independent air force. In 1921 and 1922 Mitchell arranged for planes to bomb and sink several warships to demonstrate his ideas. In 1925 Mitchell was court-martialed (tried by a military court; MacArthur was a member of the court) for his outspoken criticism of U.S. military officers. Mitchell was found guilty and suspended from the army without pay for five years. He resigned the following year, but continued to promote his vision of an independent air force. Mitchell's ideas were adopted during World War II.

MacArthur launched a daring amphibious landing (delivery of ground troops by sea) of UN troops at Inchon on the west coast. The landing was a brilliant success, and the North Korean army retreated.

Pushing the North Koreans beyond the 38th parallel back into their own country was the best way to eliminate the threat to South Korea. According to the UN plan, however, UN forces were to wage only a limited war. They could run North Korea out of the south, and nothing more. If UN forces went beyond the 38th parallel they would be in violation of the UN charter (an agreement signed by the original UN members that defined the organization's role, duties, and limits). At that point, politics entered the picture.

Communism a threat

During the early 1950s the United States was in the midst of anti-communist hysteria (see "Society" entry). (Communism is a political philosophy that advocates state ownership of all property and control of all social services and industrial operations.) Fearful U.S. politicians warned that, as a communist country, North Korea remained a threat to non-communist South Korea. Moreover, China—North Korea's giant communist neighbor to the north—was an even bigger threat, not only to Asia but also to Europe. Since the UN strike had been so effective in South Korea, the politicians argued, the job should be completed with the destruction of communist military bases above the 38th parallel.

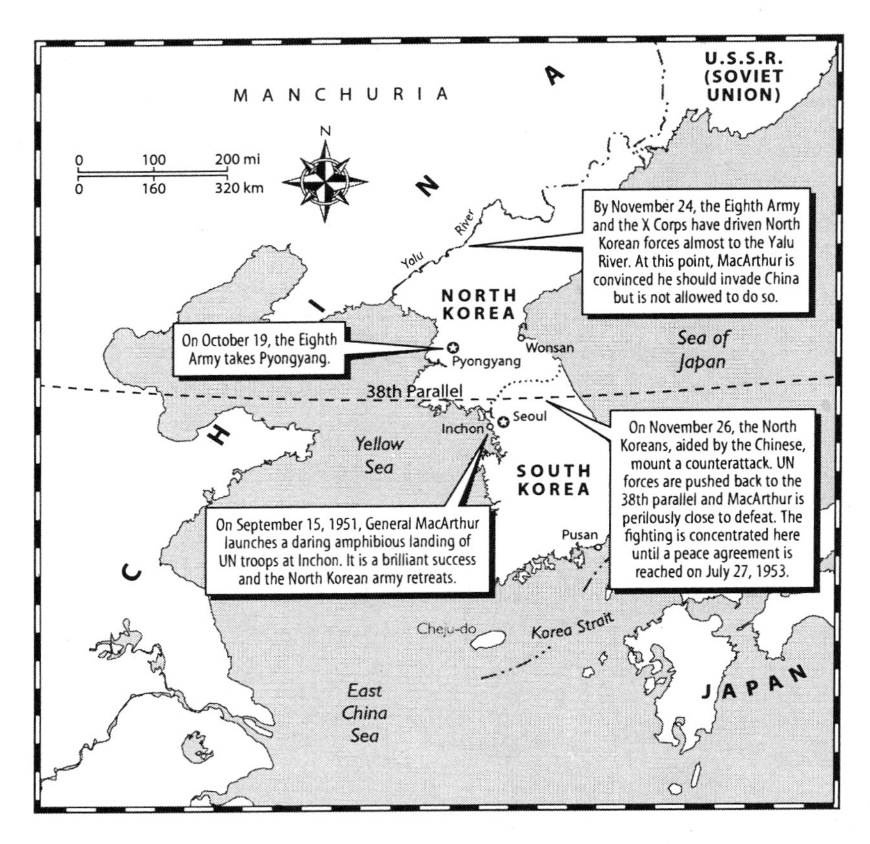

The Korean War broke out in 1951 after the communist government of North Korea invaded South Korea.

An avid anticommunist himself, MacArthur encouraged this position in discussions with Truman's advisors. Finally persuaded, Truman decided to go even further and unify Korea under the government of Syngman Rhee (1875–1965), the president of the Republic of Korea. On September 27, Truman authorized MacArthur to move north of the 38th parallel. The president specified, however, that only Korean troops should be allowed to enter the provinces on the Chinese border.

Chinese vow retaliation

On October 3, China warned that if American troops went into North Korea, the Chinese would respond with force. MacArthur shrugged off the warning as a bluff. He also boasted that he had enough troops to beat both the Chinese and the Soviet Union if they were foolish enough to go against him.

Four days later the UN issued a resolution calling for North Korea to surrender. MacArthur was authorized to cross the 38th parallel and to unify Korea by force. In response, Mao Tsetung (1893–1976), chairman of the People's Republic of China, sent troops into North Korea. Yet MacArthur was so confident of victory that he divided his forces into two prongs. He sent the Eighth Army toward the North Korean capital of Pyongyang. Then he directed the X Corps to make an amphibious landing at Wonsan, a city in North Korea on the Sea of Japan. (MacArthur called this part of the campaign "the son of Inchon.")

Back home, Truman had decided to go to Asia. He wanted to evaluate the situation himself—and to meet MacArthur for the first time—because members of the Joint Chiefs of Staff (JCS; an advisory panel consisting of the heads of all the military services) had warned him that the aging general was no longer reliable. On October 15 Truman and MacArthur met on the island of Wake in the Pacific Ocean. The general assured the president that there was no real threat of Chinese or Soviet intervention. If either or both of these nations became involved, MacArthur predicted, they would be no match for superior American power. Truman was so impressed that he gave MacArthur the Distinguished Service Medal (the general's fifth such honor) and pronounced the meeting a success.

MacArthur violates orders

On October 19 the Eighth Army took Pyongyang. The following day MacArthur announced that the war would soon be over. By November 24 the Eighth Army and the X Corps had driven North Korean forces almost to the Yalu River, which runs along the border between North Korea and Communist China. During these assaults MacArthur had violated Truman's direct orders by bombing bridges along the Yalu inside China. Making matters worse, MacArthur himself did not inform the president of his actions. When Truman learned of this development, he demanded that no bombing missions should be conducted within five miles of the Chinese border. MacArthur then threatened to resign. Reporting that Chinese forces were streaming across the river (an exaggeration), he claimed the only way to prevent the loss of American lives—and to save Europe from the Communists—was to mount bombing raids

DOUGLAS MACARTHUR

Douglas MacArthur (1880–1964) was the third son of Arthur MacArthur, a U.S. Army officer, and Mary Hardy MacArthur, a strong-willed woman who was an important influence in her son's life. In 1903 MacArthur graduated with highest honors from the United States Military Academy at West Point. During World War I (1914–18) he rose to the rank of army divisional commander. After the war he was the superintendent at West Point, where he instituted numerous important reforms. MacArthur retired from the army in 1935, but when the United States became involved in World War II he was recalled to active duty and placed in command of Allied forces in the Southwest Pacific. Following the war MacArthur headed the Allied occupation of Japan. He has been credited with initiating positive social and political changes in that country.

In 1948 MacArthur was seriously considered as a Republican candidate for the U.S. presidency, but his nomination was defeated in preliminary elections (a selection of candidates to run in final elections). At the outset of the Korean War, MacArthur was chosen to lead United Nations' forces in an attempt to prevent Communist North Korea from taking over noncommunist South Korea. After he was removed from command in Korea in 1951, he became chair of the board of the Remington Rand Corporation (1952). MacArthur then lived in seclusion in New York City, only occasionally appearing in public.

on the Yalu bridges. The JCS relented and gave MacArthur permission to continue bombing. MacArthur did not resign, and was by now convinced that he had a mandate to be "the swordsman who would slay the Communist dragon."

Wants to use atomic bombs

On November 26, as MacArthur was planning a decisive victory in Korea, the Communists mounted a counterattack. More than 300,000 Chinese and 65,000 North Korean troops swept down on UN forces. Two days later 11,000 UN soldiers were dead, and MacArthur was perilously close to defeat. UN forces were finally pushed back to the 38th parallel. (The fighting would be concentrated there for the remainder of the war, until a peace agreement was reached on July 27, 1953.) Looking for a scapegoat, the demoralized general blamed the JCS and Truman for not letting him bomb China itself. For months he had wanted to recruit Chinese Nationalist troops from Taiwan (an independent, democratic Chinese nation). He had also been urging the use of atomic bombs against China. Now

MacArthur announced publicly that one or both of these measures should be undertaken if the United Nations were to win the war and avoid losing all of Asia.

An international crisis

Truman was alarmed by MacArthur's irrational and unauthorized pronouncements. America's allies were equally shocked by the statements because they risked a war with China and endangered the welfare of Europe. The allies did not believe that communism needed to be conquered in Asia in order to save Europe. Britain threatened to lead other European nations in withdrawing support from the United States in Korea. To salvage the situation, Truman decided to retreat from the goal of unifying Korea. In January 1951 the Communists took Seoul, the capital of South Korea. This loss only fueled MacArthur's resolve to use America's atomic might. He discussed dropping twenty-six atom bombs on China in order to prevent Asia from being overtaken by the Communists. When MacArthur gained no support for his atom-bomb strategy, he offered a new plan: He would mount massive air strikes against North Korea, then lay a field of radioactive waste along the border between Korea and Manchuria (a region in northeast China) to prevent the Communists from entering by that route.

Relieved of command

In March, MacArthur threatened a full-scale invasion of China if the Communists did not agree to let Korea and Taiwan remain free nations. He further demanded that Mao Tsetung meet UN commanders face to face and admit defeat. By now European leaders were accusing Truman of having no control over MacArthur. On April 8 the JCS advised the president to fire the general. Three days later Truman announced that he had relieved MacArthur of his commands in Korea, Japan, and the Far East on charges of insubordination and an unwillingness to wage a limited war.

Gives memorable speech

Nine days later MacArthur addressed a nationally televised joint session of the U.S. Congress (both the House of Representatives and the Senate). He closed his dramatic speech with these famous lines: "The world has turned over many times since I took the oath on the plain at West Point," he said, "and the hopes and dreams have long since vanished. But I still remember the refrain from one of the most popular barracks ballads of that day, which proclaimed most profoundly that 'Old soldiers never die; they just fade away.' And like the old soldier of that ballad, I now close my military career and just fade away—an old soldier who tried to do his duty as God gave him the light to see that duty. Good-bye."

Although Truman's dismissal of MacArthur was applauded by Europeans and Asians alike, opinion in the United States was deeply divided. Many Americans felt MacArthur should have been discharged months earlier, but in the eyes of others, the general returned home a hero. A U.S. Senate investigation eventually revealed the extent of MacArthur's actions in Korea, including the unauthorized bridge bombings. Most historians now regard MacArthur as a complex person with a superior intelligence and brilliant military skills. Others contend that he had become unstable in his later years and should never have headed the campaign in Korea.

FOR FURTHER REFERENCE

Books

Finkelstein, Norman H. *The Emperor General: A Biography of Douglas MacArthur.* Minneapolis, MN: Dillon Press, 1989.

Regan, Geoffrey. *Snafu: Great American Military Disasters.* New York City: Avon Books, 1993.

The Bay of Pigs Invasion

APRIL 17, 1961

Lacking the full support of the U.S. military, the Cuban Brigade was left to confront Castro's army on its own and met defeat.

The Bay of Pigs invasion was a secret military operation planned by the U.S. Central Intelligence Agency (CIA) that caused great embarrassment and political damage to the United States. On April 17, 1961, a CIA-trained army of Cuban exiles (natives of Cuba who sought refuge in the United States) landed off the coast of Cuba. Called the Cuban Brigade, the exiles were on a mission to create an uprising among Cuban citizens against dictator Fidel Castro. Unfortunately, nothing went as planned, and the campaign turned into a huge misadventure. Lacking the full support of the U.S. military, the Brigade was left to confront Castro's army on its own and met defeat. As a result, America lost international prestige and communism gained strength in Cuba.

Castro takes over Cuba

Fidel Castro (1926–) took over Cuba in January 1959 after overthrowing dictator Fulgencio Batista (1901–1973). Within a short time after the takeover, Cuba's diplomatic ties with the United States began to weaken. The main reason for this breakdown in relations was Castro's growing interest in communism (a political philosophy that advocates state ownership of all property and control of all social services and industrial operations). As a part of his effort to transform Cuba, Castro did three

Cuban leader Fidel Castro was seen as a threat by United States officials due to his growing interest in communist ideas.

things that the U.S. government found unacceptable. First, he started to associate with countries that practiced socialism (a political philosophy that advocates responsibility for ownership, development, and distribution of property equally between members of society). Next, he began inciting revolutions in Latin-American countries. Finally, Castro began confiscating (or seizing) private property in Cuba, even though some of this land was owned by North American interests. All of these changes provoked reaction from the United States.

Cuban exiles go to U.S.

Many Cuban citizens were also disturbed by the actions of their new leader. Castro's takeover triggered a mass exodus (departure) of refugees to the United States, many of whom settled in Miami, Florida. In June 1960, the United States Congress passed a law that enabled President Dwight D. Eisenhower (1890–1969) to retaliate (fight back) against Castro's government. The following year, Eisenhower placed an embargo (ban) on all exports except for shipments of medicine and food from the United States to Cuba. He also ended all diplomatic relations (negotiations in an effort to avoid hostilities) with Cuba. When Eisenhower reached the end of his second term as president, the Cuban problem was placed in the hands of the new American president, John F. Kennedy (1917–1963).

CIA plans Cuban invasion

Kennedy came into office in 1961. By that time, the American government was heavily involved in the Cuban crisis. Not only had Eisenhower gradually broken off ties with Cuba, but he had also authorized the CIA to begin planning an invasion of the country. (The CIA is an independent bureau of the U.S. government that secretly gathers political information in foreign countries.) Since May 1960 the CIA had been secretly training anti-Castro Cuban exiles in Guatemala (a country in Central

America). Although Kennedy wanted to stop the project, he reluctantly approved it on the advice of CIA supporters. Due to the delicacy of the training mission, however, President Kennedy insisted that CIA operatives remain behind the scenes.

The CIA's secret plan was to land 1,400 heavily armed Cuban exiles in Cuba to support anti-Castro rebels who were still in the country. As the exiles were landing, air strikes would be carried out by sixteen old B-26 bombers supplied by the United States but flown by Cuban refugees. The planes would take-off from bases in Nicaragua (a country in Central America, southwest from Cuba across the Caribbean Sea). According to the strategy, the B-26s would destroy Castro's air force, then remain to assist in the landing. Once on shore, the ground troops would be joined by Cuban rebels already in the country. After toppling the Castro regime, the exiles and rebels would form a new government that would be openly assisted by the United States. The most important feature of the plan was that the United States would provide U.S. equipment and technical assistance, but no troops, for the invasion.

President John F. Kennedy reluctantly agreed to the Bay of Pigs mission on the advice of CIA operatives.

Mission doomed

The invasion was doomed almost from the start. On April 14, 1961, the Cuban Brigade set sail from Nicaragua aboard five small freighters (cargo ships). The Cuban captains of the ships had been trained by the CIA for the secret mission. The mission was so secret, in fact, that the navigation charts were sealed in envelopes the CIA had instructed the captains to open only when they were at sea. When one captain opened his envelope, however, he found that two charts were missing. Weapons were also poorly prepared. As a ship officer was testing a machine gun that had been improperly mounted, it fired onto the crew. One man was killed and several others were wounded.

Three days later, on April 17, the Cuban Brigade arrived off the coast of Cuba. The men landed at several sites, the main location being the Bay of Pigs (also called Bahía de los Cochinos) on the southwest coast. Immediately the Brigade encountered problems. Near the resort town of Playa Giron, for example, two ships ran into dangerous coral deposits that the CIA had never mentioned in its reports. As the ships ran up onto the coral, they were badly damaged and troops were flung into the sea.

An even worse ordeal lay ahead. Castro's army was stronger than anyone had expected and, more crucially, there was no uprising of Cuban citizens against their new leader. The success of the invasion hinged entirely upon the Cuban Brigade joining forces with anti-Castro groups already in the country. The CIA had convinced Kennedy's advisers that 2,500 rebels would be waiting, and that at least 20,000 more men would rally to the cause. The CIA further predicted that fully twenty-five percent of the Cuban population would support the invasion. Now that there was no outpouring of massive reinforcements, the small band of 1,400 troops (only 135 of whom had actual military experience) was left to wage the battle alone. They were no match for Castro's army, which numbered more than 200,000 men.

In addition to not anticipating a large opposing force, the Brigade were led to believe that Castro's air force was weak. The B-26 air strikes carried out before the troop landing were to have destroyed most of the remaining Cuban planes. This was not the case. Kennedy was so uncertain about the entire operation that he had canceled the last air attack. When the Brigade reached Cuba, they received a message from Miami informing them that some of Castro's planes were still intact. As the B-26s provided air support for troops fanning out onto the island, the Cuban air force fought back with surprising force.

Invasion fails

Before the invasion, American officials were so worried about their involvement in the conflict that they had trained Cuban pilots instead of American pilots to fly the slow-moving American B-26 fighter planes. After confronting Castro's forces, however, the Cuban Brigade pilots were too tired to fly; as a result they were replaced by American pilots hired by the CIA. Eventually, Kennedy relented and sent in reinforcements. He ordered six unmarked planes from the *Essex*, an American car-

FALLEN PILOTS HONORED

The CIA recruited a number of pilots to fly decrepit B-26 bombers in the April 1961 invasion of Cuba. Four of these pilots died in action. According to standard CIA secrecy precautions, however, the pilots' bodies were never recovered. Among the dead was Thomas (Pete) Ray, who had a six-year-old daughter named Janet. For years Janet wondered what had really happened to her father during the invasion. According to the CIA, Ray was a mercenary (professional soldier) hired by wealthy Cuban exiles (people who live outside their own country for political reasons) who drowned when his plane went into the ocean. Janet was never convinced by this story. After she married and became Janet Weininger, she began looking for answers. When the CIA gave her no assistance, Weininger wrote to Fidel Castro. The Cuban leader responded that her father was killed after his plane was shot down over Cuba, and his body had been kept in a refrigerator in Havana.

In 1979, Weininger arranged to bring Ray's body back for burial in the United States. Largely through Weininger's efforts the CIA officially recognized the contributions of Thomas Ray and the three other American pilots nearly two decades later. In May 1998, the CIA honored the men by placing four stars on the wall of the lobby at the agency's headquarters in Langley, Virginia. (A total of seventy-one stars represent agents and others, many of them anonymous, who lost their lives during CIA missions.) The pilots' names were also entered in a "Book of Honor" located in a glass case below the stars.

rier (a ship that serves as a base for fighter planes) in the waters off Cuba, to assist the B-26 fighters that were still in Nicaragua. With this kind of backup, the Brigade invasion might have been successful, if not for one final mistake. When the planes took off from their respective locations on the *Essex* and in Nicaragua, no one had stopped to consider that Cuba and Nicaragua were in different time zones. As a result, the B-26 fighters arrived one hour before their reinforcements from Nicaragua. Outnumbered by the Cuban air force, four B-26 fighters were shot down by Cuban T-33 planes. The Bay of Pigs invasion was over.

U.S. responsible for failure

The Bay of Pigs fiasco had lasted only sixty-four hours. As soon as the B-26 fighter planes were shot down, Cuban Brigade ground troops were overwhelmed by Castro's army. In the end, 114 Brigade members were killed and 1,189 were captured and taken to Havana (the capital of Cuba) as prisoners. After the invasion was over, a shocked President Kennedy wondered how the operation could have been such a disaster. There were no easy answers for him or the American public.

In the eyes of many Americans, the mission's greatest failure was a loss in their country's international status. If government officials had not been so concerned about maintaining secrecy, they could have offered more military support to the Cuban exiles. By many historians' estimation, Castro's army would have been no match against a well-planned and supported American military effort. The unwillingness of the U.S. government to lend more support led to another failure: a loss of faith. The Cuban exiles knew that they were taking a major risk in returning to their home country as an armed force, but they believed the United States would not let them down. In fact, CIA advisers had promised the Cuban exiles that they could count on U.S. troops joining them within seventy-two hours after the Cuban Brigade's first unit landed. That promise, however, was never fulfilled.

Communism now close to U.S.

After the invasion, American officials became very concerned that the threat of communism was now within striking distance of the United States. Castro's new regime was heavily backed and endorsed by the Soviet Union, a major communist power. The Soviets were happy to witness an American military failure, in large part because it strengthened Soviet standing in the Cold War. (The Cold War was a period of nonaggressive hostilities between Western powers and Soviet Communist countries that began after the end of World War II [1939–45] and continued until 1989, when the Soviet Union was dissolved.) The Bay of Pigs disaster was crucial to the development of the Cuban missile crisis in October 1962, when the Soviet Union threatened to build missile bases in Cuba.

The Cuban missile crisis

In the summer of 1962, Soviet premier Nikita Khrushchev (1894–1971) ordered the secret installation of ballistic missiles in Cuba. (A ballistic missile is launched by rocket from a base on land.) Shortly thereafter, U.S. spy planes took pictures of the missile launching sites as they were under construction. On

October 22, 1961, President Kennedy publicly criticized the Soviet Union's actions. He then sent U.S. ships to form a blockade, or barrier, around Cuba. Kennedy warned that if a missile was fired from Cuba the United States would take full-scale military action against the Soviet Union. On October 24, Soviet ships that were taking missiles to Cuba turned back toward Russia. Four days later Krushchev agreed to remove missiles and dismantle the launch sites. The United States ended the blockade of Cuba on November 20, the Soviets withdrew the missiles, and the crisis was over before the new year.

FOR FURTHER REFERENCE

Books

Higgins, Trumbull. *The Perfect Failure: Kennedy, Eisenhower, and the Bay of Pigs.* New York City: Norton, 1987.

Periodicals

Thomas, Ewan. "On the Trail of the Truth." *Newsweek.* May 11, 1998, p. 38.

The Vietnam War

1961 TO 1973

The media, especially television, played a major role in exposing the Vietnam War as a tragic misadventure.

The Vietnam War, which spanned the administrations of four U.S. presidents, was one of the most disastrous military engagements in American history. The United States entered the conflict in the 1950s in an advisory capacity, aiding the government of South Vietnam against Viet Cong guerilla forces supported by communist North Vietnam. By 1966 U.S. involvement had escalated to a full-scale commitment of troops, equipment, and economic aid in the fight against Communist aggression. The war soon became a catastrophe for U.S. government and military leaders, who tried to claim victory in South Vietnam in spite of failing to suppress the insurgents from the north. The media, especially television, played a major role in exposing the Vietnam War as a tragic misadventure. Each evening Americans watched images of death and destruction flash across their television screens. Public backlash against the U.S. presence in Vietnam began in 1967, gaining momentum until American troops were finally withdrawn in 1973.

Fear of communist aggression

United States involvement in Vietnam dated back to the French Indochina War (1946–54). France had controlled commercial interests in Vietnam since the nineteenth century, and the war broke out when communist China tried to occupy the country. At the same time Americans were gripped by an intense fear of communism (a political philosophy that advocates state ownership of all property and control of all social services and industrial operations; see McCarthy and Rosenberg entries in "Society"). The U.S. government supported the French effort against China—in fact, by 1950 the United States was paying eighty percent of French military costs. In 1954 communist Vietnamese forces, backed by China and the Soviet Union (also a communist nation), defeated the French at the battle of Dienbienphu.

United States in South Vietnam

As a result of the communist victory, in 1954 the Geneva Accords temporarily divided the country into the communist Democratic Republic of Vietnam (North Vietnam) and the noncommunist Republic of Vietnam (South Vietnam). Free elections for the unification of Vietnam under a single government were scheduled to be held in South Vietnam in 1956. South Vietnamese President Ngo Dinh Diem (1901–1963) canceled the elections when he realized the Communists would probably win. Diem was then criticized by Ho Chi Minh (1890–1969), the president of North Vietnam. Diem's government faced intensifying opposition from the Viet Cong, guerilla forces trained in Hanoi, the capital of North Vietnam. (Guerillas are soldiers who use unconventional fighting strategies that include ambush.) Alarmed at the prospect of communism spreading throughout Asia, the administration of U.S. President Dwight D. Eisenhower (1890–1969) backed Diem with advisory assistance and military aid. The goal was to build up the Army of the Republic of Vietnam (ARVN).

In 1960 the Viet Cong established a political organization, the National Front for the Liberation of Vietnam (NLF), which further strengthened communist infiltration in the south. Finally, unable to oust the guerillas, South Vietnam signed a formal treaty with the United States in 1961. Within a year, during the administration of President John F. Kennedy (1917–1963), the number of U.S. military advisers in South Vietnam had grown to 11,000 people (from a 1960 level of 900). Diem became increasingly unpopular among his own people, however, and on November 1, 1963, he was assassi-

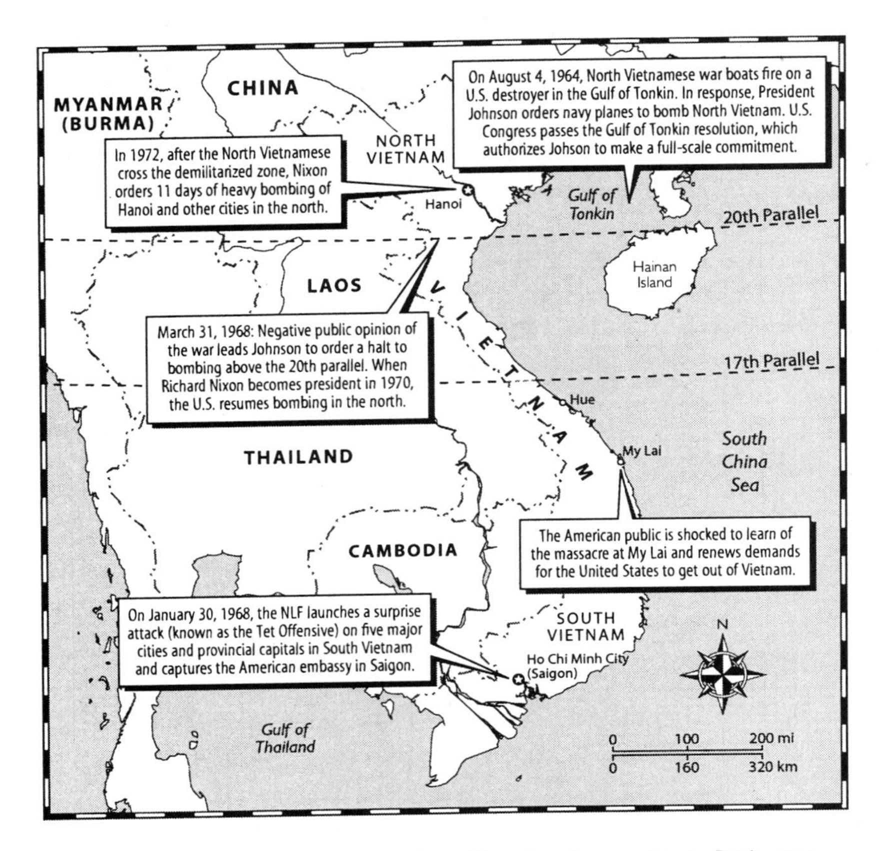

The Vietnam War spanned the administrations of four American presidents. By the time the last U.S. troops withdrew from the country in 1973, over 50,000 lives had been lost.

nated in a military coup (an overthrow of the government by military forces).

Gulf of Tonkin Resolution

Three weeks later Kennedy was also assassinated, and Vice President Lyndon B. Johnson (1908–1973) was sworn in as president. As the conflict intensified, the United States continued its support of the ARVN. Then on August 4, 1964, North Vietnamese war boats fired on the U.S. destroyer *Maddox* (a small warship equipped with guns and missiles) in the Gulf of Tonkin (an arm of the China Sea east of North Vietnam). In response, Johnson ordered navy planes to bomb North Vietnam. The U.S. Congress immediately passed the Gulf of Tonkin Resolution, which authorized Johnson to make a full-scale U.S. commitment.

In the meantime, 400,000 ARVN soldiers had been losing the war against 35,000 NLF troops, who were receiving arms and assistance from the Soviet Union and other communist countries. At this point the United States was pledged not only to assisting South Vietnam, but also to showing other Western nations that Americans would lead the fight against communist aggression. By 1967, 389,000 U.S. troops, under the command of General William C. Westmoreland (1914–), were in Vietnam.

Massive Agent Orange spraying

In spite of deploying the most sophisticated weapons and equipment, American and South Vietnamese forces were no match for the enemies from the north. The main problem was that U.S. ground troops and helicopter and bomber pilots were not prepared to fight against the Viet Cong guerillas. Much of Vietnam is covered by dense forests and jungles, so the Viet Cong could easily hide in the underbrush and launch surprise attacks. It was extremely difficult to locate the guerillas, and communication between U.S. and ARVN troops was nearly impossible.

As early as 1960 the South Vietnamese government requested that the United States spray defoliants (chemicals that kill the leaves of plants and trees; also called herbicides) to clear the jungles and forests of vegetation. In 1962 the military found that Agent Orange (see "Science and Technology" entry) was the most effective defoliant. By 1965 Agent Orange was being sprayed in massive quantities. In the case of dense jungle growth, planes sprayed two applications of the herbicide—one for the upper layers of vegetation and the other for the lower layers. The use of Agent Orange continued until 1971. Only later, nearly two decades after the war had ended, did U.S. government and military leaders acknowledge that these heavy saturations had poisoned American soldiers as well as South Vietnamese troops and civilians.

Antiwar sentiment grows

A turning point in the war came during the Tet (new year) festival. In observance of the holiday, a truce (a temporary halt in fighting) had been declared. Nevertheless, on January 30, 1968, the NLF launched a surprise attack on five major cities and thirty-six provincial capitals in South Vietnam. For a month, amid fierce fighting known as the "Tet Offensive," the NLF held Saigon (the capital of South Vietnam) and the city of Hue (pronounced "hway"). U.S. and ARVN troops finally defeated the NLF, which sustained heavy casualties. U.S. officials claimed to be winning the struggle, and Westmoreland asked for more troops in order to retain control and gain a definitive victory.

In spite of the apparent success of U.S. strategy, Americans had turned against continued involvement in Vietnam. Opposition to the war had been building since 1967, as citizens and politicians questioned whether the United States could actually win in Vietnam. Many people were skeptical about the morality of intervening in a civil war in a foreign country. Several politicians led the antiwar movement, including Senators James William Fulbright (born in 1905), Robert F. Kennedy (1925–1968), Eugene J. McCarthy (1916–), and George S. McGovern (1922–). Hundreds of thousands of citizens joined the opposition, demanding "de-escalation" in Vietnam. People organized peace marches, committed acts of civil disobedience (nonviolent opposition to government policy), and staged mass demonstrations on college campuses and in major cities.

First "television war"

The media—television, newspapers, and magazines—played a major role in generating public discontent. Television in particular had a powerful impact; in fact, the Vietnam War came to be known as the first "television war." Before the Tet Offensive, television commentators had presented standard images of troops trampling through thick jungles as helicopters hovered overhead and warplanes bombed villages in the distance. Although viewers were routinely informed of body counts (the number of people killed), they were essentially removed from the everyday horrors of war. When the Viet Cong seized part of the American embassy in Saigon during the Tet Offensive, however, television networks beamed on-the-spot, full-color reports into homes throughout the nation. Americans were given close-up views of U.S. soldiers shooting at Viet Cong guerillas. They saw the bodies of the dead and wounded, and they heard the continuous sounds of humming planes and rumbling bombs.

MY LAI MASSACRE On March 16, 1968, Lieutenant William L. Calley led a unit of U.S. soldiers into My Lai, a South Vietnamese village. The Americans believed My Lai was being used to harbor Viet Cong guerillas, so they started firing their weapons. According to a U.S. Army estimate, 347 unarmed civilians—mostly old men, women, and children—were killed. The American public was unaware of the incident until 1969, when a former soldier revealed the details in letters to the government. After investigations by the army and the U.S. House of Representatives, many soldiers and veterans were charged with murder and several officers were accused of dereliction (neglect) of duty. Five soldiers were finally charged, but only Calley was convicted. Found guilty of murdering twenty-two Vietnamese civilians, he was sentenced to life in prison on March 29, 1971. (A federal court overturned the conviction in 1974.) Although the army released Calley, it appealed the court's decision.

Thirty years after the My Lai massacre, three U.S. soldiers were honored for risking their lives to save Vietnamese civilians. On the day of the incident, pilot Hugh Thompson, door-gunner Lawrence Colbern, and crew chief Glenn Andreotta were flying their helicopter over My Lai. Down below, they saw American troops killing Vietnamese people. Landing the aircraft between the soldiers and the fleeing civilians, the three men pointed their guns at the soldiers to prevent further killing. As Colbern and Andreotta continued to keep the soldiers at gunpoint, Thompson confronted the leader of the shooters. He also persuaded a group of Vietnamese to come out of a building so he could transport them to safety.

Andreotta died in battle three weeks after the incident at My Lai. On March 7, 1998, Thompson, Colburn, and Andreotta were honored with the Soldier's Medal, the highest award for bravery not involving conflict with an enemy. The ceremony was held at the Vietnam Veterans' Memorial, where Andreotta's name is etched on panel 48-E.

The U.S. won back the embassy in six hours, and Westmoreland stood before reporters amid the smoking rubble to proclaim victory. Americans were not wholly convinced, however, that the victory was worth the cost. After Tet, body counts took on a different meaning—real human beings, not mere statistics, were dying in the fighting. Newspapers and magazines picked up on the public's growing sense of horror. Soon reporters and news analysts were questioning Westmoreland's military strategy. Although the Viet Cong had been defeated, they pointed out, television had shown that the guerillas were putting up a good fight. Even worse, Westmoreland's optimism was exposed as a lie because television reports revealed that the

South Vietnamese army was weak and probably would not hold out much longer.

War drags on

Public opinion forced Johnson to take decisive action. On March 31, 1968, in a nationally televised address, he ordered a halt to bombing above the 20th parallel in Vietnam. He also announced that he would not seek reelection. Within months, the bombing stopped completely. After Communist leaders in Hanoi withdrew troops from the south, peace talks began in Paris, France, between the United States and North Vietnam. General Creighton Abrams (1914–1974) was placed in command of American forces in South Vietnam. Within a year South Vietnam and the NLF were included in the peace talks.

In 1970, after Richard M. Nixon (1913–1996) became president, the United States resumed bombing in the north. The Viet Cong seemed to have an endless supply of troops, who continued to infiltrate the south. U.S. military leaders eventually concluded that while they withdrew troops (about 160,000 U.S. military personnel remained), they would make bombing raids into North Vietnam to cut off the Viet Cong. Then U.S. forces would invade Viet Cong sanctuaries (safe areas) in neighboring Cambodia.

By 1970 the United States had been in Vietnam for at least fourteen years and actively fighting for nine of those years. Americans were alarmed to see the war expanding rather than ending. U.S. casualties were high, and the public was shocked to learn that the United States was involved in war crimes such as the massacre at My Lai. Weary of the war, the public renewed demands for the United States to get out of Vietnam. Even as the war continued, peace talks in Paris moved ahead, with Henry Kissinger (1923–) as the U.S. negotiator. In 1972, after the North Vietnamese crossed the demilitarized zone (a neutral area where no fighting was to take place), Nixon ordered eleven days of heavy bombing of Hanoi and other cities in the north.

U.S. troops withdrawn

A peace agreement was finally signed on January 27, 1973, by the United States, North Vietnam, South Vietnam,

VIETNAM ON FILM The Vietnam War was the inspiration for some of the most critically-acclaimed films ever made in the United States. These films include *The Deer Hunter* (1978), *Apocalypse Now* (1979), and *Born on the Fourth of July* (1989). *The Deer Hunter* and *Apocalypse Now*, each of which won several Academy Awards, are powerful fictional portrayals of American soldiers' experiences in the war. *Born on the Fourth of July* was adapted from the best-selling autobiography by Ron Kovic, a disabled Vietnam War veteran. All three films are available on videocassette recording.

and the NLF provisional revolutionary government. According to the treaty, hostilities would end and all U.S. and allied forces would be withdrawn. (In addition to the United States and South Vietnam, the allies included troops from several Southeast Asia Treaty Organization countries.) Both sides would exchange prisoners, and a four-nation international control commission would enforce the treaty. The following August, the U.S. Congress passed a resolution against any further involvement by the United States in Indochina (Vietnam and neighboring countries).

By the end of 1973 very few U.S. military personnel were still in South Vietnam. Fighting between South Vietnam and North Vietnam continued until 1975, when North Vietnam captured Saigon. Vietnam was formally reunified under communist rule in July 1976, and Saigon was later renamed Ho Chi Minh City. American casualties in Vietnam during the period of active U.S. involvement (1961 to 1973) numbered over 50,000. Over 400,000 South Vietnamese lost their lives, and Viet Cong and North Vietnamese casualties were estimated to be more than 900,000.

Pain lingers

The fact that Vietnam was reunified under communist rule made the war an even worse disaster for many Americans. The United States had always won its wars, and in this case the mightiest military force in the world turned out to be the "loser." Large numbers of Vietnam veterans had difficulty adjusting to life back home, not only due to physical and psychological trauma, but also because many Americans were openly opposed to the war effort. For many veterans, Ameri-

Maya Lin's design for the Vietnam Veterans' Memorial originally caused a great deal of controversy. Over the years, however, the stone monument has become one of the most visited sites in the nation's capital.

cans either seemed to want to forget Vietnam or blame the horrors of the war on the men who fought it.

Even the Vietnam Veterans' Memorial, designed by architect Maya Lin (1959–), became a source of controversy. The now-famous monument consists of two highly polished walls of black granite set in a V-shape and inscribed with the names of dead or missing Vietnam veterans. Some veterans and their families were unhappy with Lin's concept. They felt that it was too plain and did not reflect the heroism of the soldiers who fought in the war. Protestors successfully petitioned for an additional design by sculptor Frederick Hart. Hart's bronze sculpture of three servicemen with an American flag was placed one hundred and twenty feet away from the wall, near the entrance to the memorial. The Vietnam Veterans' Memorial was dedicated on November 12, 1982. Over the years, it has become the most popular monument in the nation's capital.

Veterans charge Agent Orange exposure

By the 1990s Vietnam veterans were suffering from other serious effects of the war. During the intensive defoliant spraying from 1962 until 1971, American soldiers—along with South Vietnamese civilians and soldiers—were exposed to dangerously high levels of Agent Orange. The toxic (poisonous) chemical contaminated the troops' food and water supplies. After the war, veterans charged that their children were born with birth defects and they themselves were suffering from cancers and other diseases directly linked to use of the herbicide. The U.S. government and the chemical companies that made Agent Orange vigorously fought the veterans' claims. The full story of the Agent Orange tragedy gradually began to unfold, but the government did not acknowledge its role until 1993—twenty years after the U.S. military withdrew from Vietnam.

FOR FURTHER REFERENCE

Books

Barr, Roger. *The Vietnam War.* San Diego, CA: Lucent Books, 1991.

Capps, Walter. *A Vietnam Reader.* New York City: Routledge, 1991.

Periodicals

"Three Honored for Saving Lives at My Lai." *The New York Times.* March 7, 1998.

Other

Vietnam, A Television History. [Videocassette] Public Broadcasting Service (PBS-TV), 1996.

Operation Eagle Claw

APRIL 24 TO APRIL 25, 1980

Contrary to President Carter's expectations, eight American lives were lost when the mission fell apart in the desert.

On April 25, 1980, American television viewers watched in horror as a Shiite Muslim holy man, the Ayatollah Khalkali, poked around in the rubble of a burned-out U.S. military helicopter. Moving closer to the camera, the Ayatollah held up the forearm and charred skull of a dead American soldier. The soldier had been sent with other U.S. troops to Tehran, Iran, on a mission to rescue sixty-six Americans being held hostage in the United States embassy. Known as "Operation Eagle Claw," the mission had been approved by President Jimmy Carter (1924–) as the most peaceful resolution to the hostage situation. Carter wanted a "quick, incisive, surgical" recovery, with "no loss of American lives" and "minimal suffering to the Iranian people themselves." The plan was set in motion but, contrary to the president's expectations, eight American lives were lost when the mission fell apart in the desert.

Hostages seized

On Sunday, November 4, 1979, the American embassy in Tehran was seized by 3,000 followers of the Shiite Muslim Ayatollah (supreme leader) Ruhollah Khomeini (1900–1989). (Shiite Muslims belong to a branch of the Islam religion that claim Ali—the cousin of Islam founder Muhammad—as the

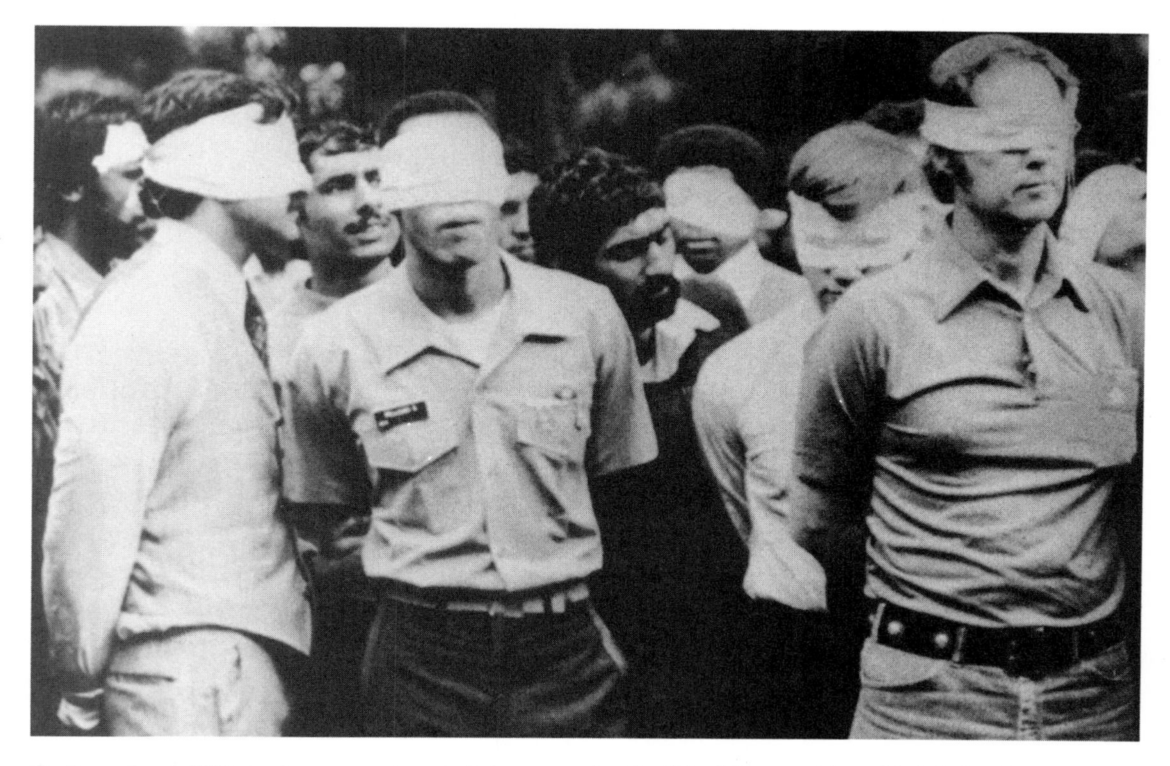

On November 4, 1979, the American embassy in Tehran was seized by Shiite followers of Ayatollah Ruhollah Khomeini. The Shiites took sixty-six people hostage and demanded the return of the former shah.

rightful head of the Islamic state.) Khomeini called the United States the "Great Satan." Taking sixty-six American hostages, the Shiites demanded the return of the shah (head of state) of Iran, Muhammad Reza Shah Pahlevi (1919–1980). The shah was in exile in Egypt and his former countrymen wanted him to be put on trial for his pro-Western policies. Khomeini's initial release of women and black men led U.S. officials to believe he was faltering or would let the rest of the hostages go free under threat of U.S. military action. Neither of these scenarios, however, would unfold.

The United States could not carry out the threat of military action for a variety of reasons, but two arguments were specifically associated with the Soviet Union. The Soviet Union was the United States' primary antagonist during the extended Cold War tensions. (The Cold War was a period of nonaggressive hostilities between Western powers and Soviet Communist countries that began after the end of World War II [1939–45] and continued until 1989, when the Soviet Union was dissolved.) By 1979 the Soviet-American relationship was extremely strained, and it was not known to what extent the Soviets would intervene if the United States attacked Iranian forces.

Also associated with the decline of the U.S.-Soviet relationship was the position of Iran, which had stood as a block against Soviet expansion toward the Persian Gulf (an arm of the Arabian Sea) and the Middle East (a region comprising countries of southwest Asia and northeast Africa). These areas were rich in oil, which was important to the economies of Japan and many European countries (most of which belonged to the North Atlantic Treaty Organization, or NATO). The United States could not count on its NATO allies for military support because such help might jeopardize these nations' access to critical oil supplies. The president could also not expect much support from the American people, who had the memory of Vietnam (see "Military" entry) still fresh in their minds.

Operation Eagle Claw

By March 22, 1980, U.S. officials realized that they were no closer to a diplomatic solution (the handling of affairs without initiating hostilities) in Iran than they had been at the start. With the threat of war no longer an option, an aggressive plan was made to go into the U.S. embassy and rescue the hostages with no loss of American lives and little threat to the people of Iran. Cyrus Vance (1917–), the secretary of state, was openly opposed to the mission. After meeting with mission commanders General James Vaught and Colonel Charles "Charging Charlie" Beckwith, however, the president was reassured by the commanders' close attention to detail. Carter approved the start of the operation on April 24, 1980.

According to the plan, Operation Eagle Claw would be carried out by eight twin-engine Sea Stallion helicopters (or choppers) aboard the U.S. carrier *Nimitz*. (A carrier is a ship that serves as a base for military aircraft.) The *Nimitz* was commanded by Lieutenant Colonel Edward R. Seiffert. The helicopters would fly to a rendezvous (meeting) point at a site called Desert Base One in the Iranian desert. Once there, the choppers would land, refuel, and then fly the troops to the Iranian capital. In the meantime, several miles away, additional troops would be boarding six four-engine C-130 transport planes that contained equipment and fuel. The lead plane would carry transport commander Colonel James H. Kyle and ground force commander Beckwith to the base. Departure went smoothly and U.S. forces arrived safely at Desert Base One.

Mishap at Desert Base One

Desert Base One was far away from habitation. Although a highway was located nearby, the site was rarely used; in fact, it had been chosen for exactly this reason. Just as the American planes landed, however, an old bus with forty-four Iranian peasants (mostly women and children) came down the road. Whether or not the driver noticed the American presence, he did not stop for the U.S. road watch team. With no other option, the team fired their guns and blew out the bus's tires and radiator. The soldiers then held the passengers and driver at gunpoint and urged everyone off the bus. Surprisingly, the Iranians showed little concern over the Americans' actions. Shortly thereafter, a fuel tanker came down the highway traveling at high speed and knocked over the American checkpoints (roadblocks set up for checking vehicles). The tanker then burst into flames. The driver, a suspected gasoline smuggler, escaped and ran across the desert to an waiting truck. The Americans assumed their operation was still safe because the smuggler would keep quiet to avoid his own arrest.

Problems with helicopters

The Sea Stallion helicopters from the *Nimitz* were scheduled to arrive at any minute. Although the helicopters were a vital part of the operation, little attention had been given to problems that could arise, such as instrument malfunction or mechanical failure. Because of the radio silence surrounding the mission, Beckwith had no idea that things were already starting to go wrong.

Miles across the desert, the helicopters were taking off. Almost immediately the pilot of chopper number eight began to have trouble operating the rotor gearbox (the instrument that controls the rotor blade, or propeller, on top of the helicopter). Then the crew of chopper six was forced to land and leave the helicopter because the craft had a damaged rotor blade. (In spite of mechanical difficulties, chopper eight was eventually able to rescue the chopper six crew.) Adding to the mechanical problems was the stress of flying 100 feet above the desert floor, which required careful concentration.

Mission canceled

In addition to the mechanical problems and the stressful conditions, the pilots encountered haboobs (clouds of sand and dust) that they had not been warned about. The pilots had to maneuver through the haboobs, which became more severe because the helicopters were hovering so close to the ground. The temperature also rose inside the helicopters and made it difficult for the pilots to breathe. Chopper five was forced to return to the *Nimitz* when its instruments malfunctioned and could not be repaired. The operation was now down to six helicopters, the minimum number needed for a successful mission.

As the six pilots landed their choppers at Desert Base One, they relayed their frustration and exhaustion to Beckwith. By now another of the helicopters was having hydraulic (water or oil pressure) problems, and it probably could not complete the mission. The experienced pilots were hesitant about continuing, and the decision to proceed was left with Beckwith. He and Kyle contacted operation commander Vaught in Egypt and explained the danger of going ahead. Although Beckwith tried to concentrate on the positive aspects of the venture, he finally followed his instincts and aborted the mission (canceled before completion). Operation Eagle Claw would not end, however, without the loss of lives.

Disaster strikes

As the helicopters prepared to return to the *Nimitz*, chopper four needed to refuel. When chopper three moved to let four pass, a gust of wind picked it up and dropped it on top of a nearby C-130 transport plane. The blades of the chopper cut through the C-130 and both the plane and the chopper burst into flames. Eight American servicemen were killed and five were seriously injured in the blast. In the panic that followed, the Americans evacuated Desert Base One, abandoning the helicopters and leaving behind secret maps and equipment. Carter was given the devastating news at 5:58 P.M.

Operation Eagle Claw had been based on the premise that no American lives should be lost, and it failed. The disaster

THE IRAN-CONTRA AFFAIR

After 444 days in captivity, the Iran hostages were released on January 20, 1981, the day of the inauguration of President Ronald Reagan. By the time Reagan was into his second term in office, however, his administration was embroiled in the Iran-Contra affair, a misadventure that had far-reaching consequences. During the 1980s several of Reagan's associates devised a secret plan to aid a guerilla war being fought by Contra rebels against the communist Sandinista government in Nicaragua. (Guerrillas are soldiers who use unconventional fighting strategies that include ambush.) To raise money for the Contras, the U.S. officials made a deal to sell arms to Iran in exchange for the release of hostages held by pro-Iranian groups in Lebanon. Profits from the sale would then be sent to the Contras. But this arrangement violated U.S. laws, which prohibited the Defense Department, the Central Intelligence Agency (CIA), or any other government agency from aiding the Contras. Reagan's men ran the arms deal through the president's National Security Council (NSC), which was not under the control of Congress. Robert McFarlane and John Poindexter raised private and foreign funds. Marine colonel Oliver North (1943–), an NSC staff member, was put in charge of delivering the arms.

In 1986 Lebanese newspapers revealed details of the arms deal, forcing the Reagan administration to admit to the plot. Poindexter resigned and North was fired. An investigation was conducted by Lawrence E. Walsh, a special prosecutor (a lawyer who files legal charges) appointed by the Justice Department. Walsh brought charges against most of the Iran-Contra participants, who were ultimately found guilty. (These convictions were later overturned by higher courts.) The Iran-Contra affair caused public debate about the limits of the executive branch of the government. Many critics called for a more active congressional role in overseeing U.S. foreign relations.

took place because the plans did not take into account any malfunctions, mechanical or otherwise. Prior to the botched mission, Secretary Vance had turned in his resignation. He had no confidence in the plan, believing that the rescue team would be taking too many chances in unfriendly territory. Eight months later, on the day of the inauguration of newly elected President Ronald Reagan (1911–), all the hostages returned home safely.

Plan flawed at outset

The Holloway Special Operations Review Group was appointed to investigate the failure of Operation Eagle Claw. The committee found twenty-three factors that made the plan fall apart, ranging from the weather to mechanical malfunctions.

The overriding problem, however, was the nature of the mission itself. Tight restrictions around the operation left very little room for error, even though there were serious doubts about the success of the venture. If the mission had come apart in Tehran—the ultimate destination of the rescue team—rather than in the desert, the failure could have been even more disastrous. Many more people, both American and Iranian, could have died. The repercussions from a Soviet reaction could also have been severe. Military experts have concluded that Operation Eagle Claw should have been aborted before it even started.

FOR FURTHER REFERENCE

Books

Lawson, Don. *America Held Hostage: The Iran Hostage Crisis and the Iran-Contra Affair.* New York City: F. Watts, 1991.

The Persian Gulf War

JANUARY TO FEBRUARY 1991

The Persian Gulf War was the crowning achievement of the presidency of George Bush (1924–). The 100-hour conflict in the Persian Gulf (an arm of the Arabian Sea) pushed the president's public approval rating to ninety-one percent. In preparation for the war, Bush relied on international connections from his career as head of the Central Intelligence Agency (CIA) and as U.S. vice president under Ronald Reagan (1911–). Bush assembled a multinational fighting force (called the coalition forces) to drive the army of Iraqi leader Saddam Hussein (1937–) out of the oil-rich country of Kuwait (between Iraq and Saudi Arabia). The United States and the coalition forces easily expelled Saddam's army from Kuwait and weakened the Iraqi leader's military presence in the region. Despite this defeat, however, Saddam remained in power in Iraq. Only later were questions raised about the failure of Western diplomats to recognize Saddam's preparations to invade Kuwait. Many critics regard the Persian Gulf conflict as a misadventure because it did not totally remove Saddam from power. This view was confirmed in early 1998 when another conflict arose, this time between the United Nations and Iraq.

Many critics regard the Persian Gulf conflict as a misadventure because it did not totally remove Saddam Hussein from power.

Americans dislike Iran

The Persian Gulf War had its roots in a previous U.S. misadventure in the Middle East (a region comprising countries in

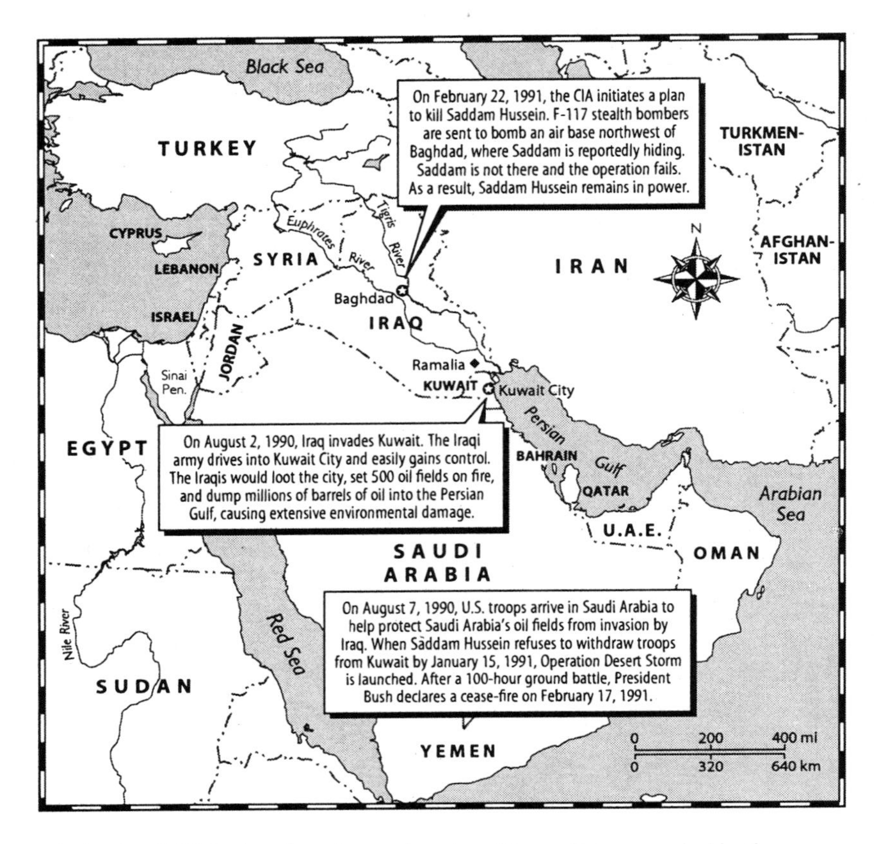

The Persian Gulf War lasted a little over four days. The conflict was marked by the coalition forces' precise use of military hardware and technology.

southeast Asia and northeast Africa). In 1979 Iranian revolutionaries overthrew the Shah (head of state) of Iran, Mohammad Reza Pahlevi (1919–1980), a strong American ally. (Shiite Muslims belong to a branch of the Islam religion that claims Ali, the cousin of Islam founder Muhammad, as the rightful head of the Islamic state.) The revolutionaries replaced the shah with the fundamentalist Shiite religious regime (or government) of the Ayatollah Ruhollah Khomeini (1900–1989).

This situation turned into a nightmare for President Jimmy Carter (1924–) when Shiite militants stormed the American embassy in Iran and took diplomats as hostages. In response, Carter approved a botched rescue attempt called Operation Eagle Claw (see "Military" entry). After the rescue attempt failed, American prestige was damaged and the Carter presidency never recovered. The situation was made worse when the Ayatollah Khomeini began calling the United States the "Great Satan" (a term for the devil, or the spirit of evil). Therefore, when Iraqi leader Saddam Hussein started a war with Iran, the United States supported him. American officials disliked Iran so much that diplomats even backed Saddam when Israel, a longtime American ally, bombed an Iraqi nuclear facility in 1981.

Fear of Shiite revolt

The Iran-Iraq war continued through the 1980s. In 1986 Iranian troops gained control of a peninsula (arm of land that reaches into a sea or ocean) twenty-five miles from Kuwait. The British and American governments saw this location as a possible staging ground for a general Shiite revolt throughout the gulf states. The Americans secretly supported the Iraqis, providing spy satellites (devices equipped with cameras that orbit the earth in space) that gave Saddam information about Iranian military bases and troop movements. When Iran criticized American involvement in the war with Iraq, no one listened. Iran lost large numbers of troops, and Iraq emerged with the world's fourth largest army. Now equipped with tanks and Scud missiles (a type of advanced long-range weapon), Iraq threatened to use nuclear or chemical weapons against Israel. Not only were Israeli diplomats now critical of Americans for backing the wrong side, but the United States also faced a major problem with Saddam.

Saddam threatens Kuwait

At the end of the eight-year Iran-Iraq war, Saddam saw himself as the defender of the Arab world against its arch-enemy, Persia (an ancient name for Iran). Since Saddam had spent most of his country's oil revenues (income) in fighting Iran, he borrowed $80 billion from Saudi Arabia and $40 billion from Kuwait. He was such a tyrant (a person who rules with absolute control), however, that neither country would ask him to repay the loans.

To make up for lost profits, Kuwait informed the Organization of Petroleum Exporting Countries (OPEC) that it planned to increase oil output by more than fifty percent. Kuwait's higher production hurt Iraq by lowering the world price of oil. Since

Iraq was completely dependent on its oil revenue, Saddam was in a tight spot. He claimed the Kuwaitis were illegally pumping from wells in Ramalia (on the Iraq-Kuwait border) and demanded all of the income from that oil. Kuwait refused and Saddam was left with two options: He could back down or he could invade Kuwait. If he backed down, his status in the Arab world would be seriously diminished.

A serious misunderstanding

On July 25, 1990, Saddam met with April Glaspie, the U.S. ambassador, to discuss the issue. Glaspie was in a difficult position. She had to show American alarm at Saddam's threats of war, but she also had to maintain good relations with Iraq. Saddam enjoyed his reputation as the tough guy of the Arab world, but he also benefitted from his relationship with the United States. Iraq was a market for American goods, and the United States could count on Saddam as an ally against Iran. According to Iraqi records of the meeting, Glaspie told Saddam that the U.S. government had "no opinion" on the border dispute with Kuwait. Saddam therefore believed he could do as he wished in Kuwait, with U.S. approval.

Operation Desert Storm: swift success

Less than two weeks later, on August 2, 1990, Iraq invaded Kuwait. The Iraqi army drove into Kuwait City and easily gained control. Saddam was confident that the United States would not become involved. On August 7, however, U.S. troops began arriving in Saudi Arabia. Known as Operation Desert Shield, this troop deployment was designed to protect Saudi oil fields from being invaded by Iraq. On November 29 the United Nations Security Council declared that Saddam had to peacefully withdraw his troops from Kuwait by January 15, 1991. Saddam refused to abide by these terms. Within three days the combined forces of thirty-two nations, under the leadership of U.S. General Norman Schwarzkopf (1943–), were launched in Operation Desert Storm.

Coalition forces succeeded in gaining control of Iraq and occupied Kuwait within a week. Saddam believed his armaments—7,000 tanks and 3,000 artillery pieces—would outnumber those held by the coalition forces. Yet his air force,

General Norman Schwarzkopf (on right; pictured here with Joint Chiefs of Staff chairman Colin Powell) headed the thirty-two-nation coalition force in Operation Desert Storm.

which had been supplied by the former Soviet Union, was seriously outmoded and therefore no match for U.S. planes and air combat technology. Unknown to Saddam, U.S. spies had also planted a virus (a computer program that destroys data) in Iraqi computers, which further disabled Saddam's already weak air defenses.

Schwarzkopf first used air power to attack the Iraqis. When Saddam foolishly ordered his army to stay fixed in the desert, Schwarzkopf then attacked the troops from behind with ground forces and tanks (armored vehicles equipped with guns that are effective in desert fighting). This tactic prevented the Iraqis from retreating. In response, Saddam launched Scud missile assaults on Israel and Saudi Arabia. He hoped that Israel would enter the war and the Arab countries would then side with Iraq, but the tactic failed.

After a 100-hour ground battle (and 150 American casualties), Bush declared a cease-fire (an end to fighting) on Febru-

A MEDIA EVENT The Persian Gulf War was a gamble on the part of U.S. president George Bush and his military advisers. Americans were deeply divided about becoming involved in a military engagement after the United States' experience in Vietnam. This long, unresolved conflict had cost over 55,000 American lives, and people were reluctant to risk the loss of life in another futile venture. An equally serious problem was that the United States had also been supporting Iraq in a war against Iran, so there was widespread confusion about the goal in attacking the army of Iraqi leader Saddam Hussein. Public opinion shifted, however, as television viewers throughout the world watched twenty-four-hour coverage of Operation Desert Storm on the Cable News Network (CNN). Spectacular live reports of the air war over Baghdad, the capital of Iraq, showed the city lit up like scenes from the movie *Star Wars*. Introducing a new era in warfare, the conflict became a popular and successful media event.

ary 17, 1991. By that time most of the Iraqi soldiers had surrendered or escaped back to Iraq. Altogether, 100,000 Iraqis died in little more than a month of fighting. The Iraqi army did the most damage in the war when they looted Kuwait City, set 500 oil fields on fire, and dumped millions of barrels of oil into the Persian Gulf. This action caused an environmental crisis in the Middle East and threatened Arab desalination plants (facilities for removing salt from sea water). The Iraqis also left the desert littered with land mines (buried explosive devices).

Diplomatic failure

The war was not completely over, however, because Saddam remained in control of Iraq and still posed a threat in the Middle East. As a final step, five days later the CIA initiated a plan to kill Saddam. F-117 stealth bombers were sent to bomb an air base northwest of Baghdad, where Saddam was reportedly hiding. The Iraqi leader, however, was not there. From a hideout somewhere in Iraq, Saddam then turned his attention to the north and waged battle with the Kurds (an ethnic group living in Iraq). U.S. political leaders were concerned about this turn of events. They wondered how Operation Desert Storm could be considered a victory if the main target—Saddam Hussein—had not been eliminated.

Glaspie was called to testify before the U.S. Congress about her meeting with Saddam. She maintained that she had told him, "We insist you settle your disputes with Kuwait nonviolently." This sentence, however, did not appear in the Iraqi transcript of the meeting. Whether Glaspie actually made the statement will never be known, but one thing is clear: Saddam was sure that American forces would not oppose his military plans.

This lapse in communication was at the heart of the diplomatic misadventure. An equally important factor was American hatred of Iran, which led Western diplomats to dismiss signs of an Iraqi threat in Kuwait. For instance, officials had seen satellite photographs of an Iraqi military buildup on the Kuwaiti border. They also saw large troop convoys (protected groups) leaving Baghdad for the south. Yet only one Pentagon (U.S. military headquarters) analyst drew the correct conclusion about Saddam's intentions, and he was ignored. Even the United Nations Security Council (the political body that monitors world conflicts)—meeting one day before Saddam's invasion—backed away from seeing the military buildup's significance.

Failure to stop Saddam

In a *Time* magazine article published in 1998, former president Bush explained why Saddam Hussein was not removed from power in the Persian Gulf War. Bush said the quick end of the war had surprised the coalition forces. Consequently, they were not prepared for drawing up peace terms and placing conditions on Saddam. Although the two main objectives—expelling Saddam from Kuwait and weakening his threat to the region—had been accomplished, other goals were harder to achieve. The Arabs told Western coalition leaders that Saddam would eventually fall as a result of his defeat. When that did not happen, diplomats hoped a revolt or coup (a military takeover) would topple his regime. Another possibility was to force Saddam himself to appear near the Kuwait-Iraq border and accept defeat. But what if he refused? Since the United States and coalition forces did not want to continue the conflict or back down on their demands, they did not require Saddam to make a personal surrender. Instead, they permitted him to send one of his generals in his place.

Lingering tensions

Vast oil reserves in the Persian Gulf—over fifty percent of the world's total oil supply—make the area a continuing source of international tension. Since Western countries rely on Arab states for oil, they are reluctant to stir up conflict. For this reason Saddam remained a threat even after the Persian Gulf War. In early 1998, for instance, he was uncooperative when the United Nations (UN) required inspections of sites in Iraq where nuclear materials were possibly being produced. Saddam accused one U.S. inspector of being a spy and expelled him from the country. Saddam also spread anti-Western propaganda in the Arab world. These actions caused worldwide concern. In response, President Bill Clinton (1946–) threatened to wage air strikes against Iraq unless Saddam agreed to cooperate with UN demands. The Iraqi leader eventually backed down, thus avoiding another war.

FOR FURTHER REFERENCE

Books

Sifry, Micah, and Christopher Cerf. *Gulf War Reader.* New York City: Times Books, 1991.

Periodicals

Bush, George, and Brent Scowcroft. "Why We Didn't Remove Saddam." *Time.* March 2, 1998.

Picture Credits

The photographs and illustrations appearing in *Great Misadventures: Bad Ideas That Led to Big Disasters* were received from the following sources:

On the cover: *Titanic* sinking (**Painting by Willie Stoewer/UPI/Corbis-Bettmann. Reproduced by permission.**).

In the text: **Corbis-Bettmann. Reproduced by permission:** 4, 19, 35, 202, 218, 241, 284, 378, 389, 410, 447, 455, 468, 544, 586, 603; **Gustave Dore/Corbis-Bettmann. Reproduced by permission:** 10; **Archive Photos. Reproduced by permission:** 16, 27, 66, 97, 150, 153, 411, 412, 418, 436, 622, 652, 725; **Library of Congress. Reproduced by permission:** 42, 48, 105, 109, 231, 372, 406, 448, 464, 494, 565, 570, 578, 581, 588, 592, 628, 651; **The Granger Collection, New York. Reproduced by permission:** 56, 76, 115, 120, 123, 158; **Charles Nahl/Corbis-Bettmann. Reproduced by permission:** 91; **AP/Wide World Photos. Reproduced by permission:** 137, 142, 166, 176, 181, 186, 193, 210, 215, 245, 249, 257, 266, 267, 275, 290, 303, 305, 335, 339, 359, 361, 363, 367, 369, 452, 503, 505, 506, 514, 518, 530, 557, 602, 605, 630, 634, 642, 644, 646, 653, 662, 673, 682, 687, 697, 700, 706, 720, 722; **Norwegian Information Services. Reproduced by permission:** 154; **Lacy Atkins. AP/Wide World Photos. Reproduced by permission:** 176; **Archive Photos/Popperfoto. Reproduced by permission:** 200; **UPI/Corbis-Bettmann. Reproduced by permission:** 205, 226, 326, 544, 547, 616, 654; **Archive Photos/Lambert. Reproduced by permission:** 211; **Lisa Bunin/Greenpeace. Reproduced by permission:** 238; **Robert Visser/Greenpeace. Reproduced by permission:** 296; **Richard Diaz. AP/Wide World Photos. Reproduced by permission:** 303; **Peter Maksymec/AP/Wide World Photos.**

Reproduced by permission: 305; Merjenburgh/Greenpeace. Reproduced by permission: 341; Peter A. Simon/Phototake. Reproduced by permission: 352; Musee de Versailles. Reproduced by permission: 426; *Harper's Weekly*/Corbis-Bettmann. Reproduced by permission: 441; National Archives and Records Administration. Reproduced by permission: 457, 459, 596, 598; Bildarchiv Preussischer Kulturbesitz. Reproduced by permission: 477; FotoMarburg/Art Resource. Reproduced by permission: 483; Michael St. Maur Sheil/Corbis-Bettmann. Reproduced by permission: 488; National Portrait Gallery. Reproduced by permission: 522; John F. Kennedy Library. Reproduced by permission: 531; Painting by J. L. Gerome/New York Public Library Picture Collection. Reproduced by permission: 562; National Baseball Library & Archive, Cooperstown, NY. Reproduced by permission: 608; Los Angeles Times Photographic Archive, Department of Special Collections, University Research Library, UCLA. Reproduced by permission: 639; The Kobal Collection. Reproduced by permission: 665; Doug Mills/AP/Wide World Photos. Reproduced by permission: 700; Junji Kurokawa/Corbis-Bettmann. Reproduced by permission: 714; Enny Nuraheni. Reuters/Archive Photos. Reproduced by permission: 725.

Index

***Italic* type indicates volume numbers; boldface type indicates entries and their page numbers; (ill.) indicates illustrations.**

A

B

C

F

G

H

I

J

K

L

M

N

O

P

Q

R

S

T

U

V

W

Y

Z